Read All About It – The Rick Bowen Story

ISBN: 978-1-914933-14-1

Published By: -

i2i Publishing. Manchester.
www.i2ipublishing.co.uk

Dedication

*For Margaret and Graham, my mum and dad, for their
unwavering love and support*

Acknowledgements

Emily Lyons, Waterside Arts Centre, Sale

Anna Stockton, Baby Cow Productions

Lily Morris, Off the Kerb Productions Limited

Richard Holton for the Cover Photograph

Jenny Weir, Editor at i2i Publishing

Lionel Ross, Proprietor & Publisher, i2i Publishing

Chapter 1

FOR someone who has spent his life trying to make himself understood, it was quite a compliment.

"You've got it," said Paul Crone, then a presenter at Granada TV.

He was referring to my interviewing technique and my ability to put people at ease.

I was at his home, interviewing him about fixtures and fittings for an 'at home with' piece for Lifestyle magazine.

The publication was set up by my employers to compete with a magazine with a similar remit, Cheshire Life.

I wrote several At Home pieces with various celebrities and quizzed them about things like interior design and general knick-knacks that caught my eye.

I even asked Paul where he bought his coffee table from. "No idea," he said. "I just put my brew on it."

A man after my own heart.

Don't get me wrong. I can appreciate items you stumble across in other people's houses from an aesthetic point of view. But my own choices tend to be guided more by whether something is, say, comfortable to sit on or does the thing I bought it to do.

Crone's compliment made such a big impression on me because I was born with cerebral palsy, a disability that affects people in a variety of different ways. In my case it affects my speech, among other things. It wasn't exactly useful when you're trying to get into a profession where good verbal communication is so important.

But I never let it become a barrier and would go on to be a successful and respected journalist.

My condition also robbed me of the ability to write in longhand and this made shorthand impossible. I could use a pen until I was 11 when my handwriting, which had always been slow, became even slower and harder to read.

So my parents came up with the bright idea of me doing my lessons at secondary school on an electric typewriter so I could keep up with my fellow pupils. The typewriter was fitted with a key guard that prevented me hitting more than one key – genius. Keyguards also fit computers and I still use them to this day.

My mum and dad have always had a philosophy that can be summed up in the phrase "there are no such things as problems, only solutions" and I'm eternally grateful to them for that.

As well as losing my ability to write, my involuntary movements became more and more obvious as I entered puberty. This was especially hard to cope with because it's the one time in your life when you're desperate to be one of the cool kids and I felt *different*.

Becoming even shakier compounded the usual pressures of adolescence, even though I'd always had a tremor, mainly in my right hand.

My eyesight also got worse which meant I needed to wear glasses from the age of 12. I felt like I was packing up already!

The neurologists I saw said the worsening of my involuntary movements were a result of my cerebral palsy getting worse and I was prescribed Valium, which is a sedative, in a bid to get them under control.

All my legal drug taking achieved was to get me in trouble in class because one of my teachers thought I was sleeping. I believe they call it 'power napping' these days.

Nearly five years ago, a doctor at the Walton Centre in Liverpool diagnosed another movement disorder - myoclonic dystonia.

People with CP – to use the trendy terminology - can develop dystonia later in life and so it was with me.

In 2017 I underwent brain surgery at the Walton in a bid to bring the symptoms of the condition under control. The operation is called deep brain stimulation – otherwise known as DBS. It works by controlling the symptoms of dystonia, so they become less apparent rather than getting rid of them.

I knew from the outset, after speaking to my surgeon and his team, there was no guarantee the DBS surgery would be a success. But I figured if I didn't give it a try, I'd spend the rest of my life wondering 'what if.'

It was very much a leap into the unknown for me, even though the surgery has been carried out on people with Parkinson's Disease for many years and four years after 'going under the knife' my treatment is very much a work in progress.

Before I started attending the Walton, I made numerous trips to see various neurologists in Manchester and I hated it.

These visits continued into early adulthood and all they did was reinforce the fact that despite spending all my waking hours surrounded by able-bodied people I wasn't and would never be exactly the same as everybody else.

While I was too immature to appreciate the doctors I saw, who were only there to help me, I found it impossible to relate to them, mainly because they were middle-aged men.

Spending most of my time surrounded by able-bodied people meant I always felt like the proverbial 'fish out of water' whenever I went on these hospital trips.

But that was a long time ago and times have changed. Compared to the 70s and 80s, when I made the majority of my hospital trips, the way the medical profession interacts with patients is much improved.

It helps being an adult of course because now I can talk to them as an equal.

So, what made me want to be a journalist?

I'd wanted to be a journalist since the age of 18 after doing a very enjoyable week's work experience at my local paper, the Sale and Altrincham Messenger.

My parents, Margaret and Graham, who have been there for me and my siblings in good times and bad, and my English teacher at secondary school, Maureen McEleney, picked up on the fact that I had a flair for the subject. Journalism seemed like a natural progression.

But initially I wasn't sure – because my verbal communication isn't as good as someone who's able-bodied.

Another reason why I was attracted to this particular profession is I felt it was something I could do where my disability, caused by a bleed on the brain at birth, didn't matter. I could leave my cerebral palsy at the office door.

So my heart sank when, shortly after joining the paper, Joan Davy, Messenger's columnist, asked if she could interview me for her weekly people profile page and included the dictionary definition of cerebral palsy in the fourth or fifth paragraph of her piece. Ah well.

The aim of the column was to interview someone with a Trafford connection who had an interesting story to tell.

Joan, who became something of an institution at the Sale and Altrincham Messenger is no longer with us.

Please don't get me wrong. I'm not ashamed of being disabled. I've just never fully accepted it and having mixed with able-bodied people I've always thought of myself as able-bodied.

Although trips to see neurologists and the verbal abuse I used to endure on the streets reminded me that I wasn't, and in my teens, there could be as many as eight incidents a week. I would sometimes go home via the back streets of Sale in a bid to avoid the piss-takers.

Some people would have hidden themselves away at home to avoid such experiences. But you're 'only young once' so the old saying goes and I wanted the same sort of social life my peers had. I wanted to go to the pubs, clubs, gigs. I wanted to get pissed, have hangovers and hopefully get laid.

Surely then, if I had stayed at home the bastards who screamed 'spacker' after me or imitated my involuntary movements would have won.

On the issue of verbal abuse, there are even occasions when other disabled people ridicule those who are more disabled than they are. I can remember attending a residential careers week at The Spastics Society in London. I shared a room with a smashing lad called Kevin who had a disability similar but more severe than my own.

Kev was highly intelligent and a really nice guy. He was trapped in a body that didn't work properly and was difficult but not impossible to understand. We got on really, really well.

But I remember losing it during a discussion group when Kevin said, "I want to make a suggestion" and one of the other lads joked "Somebody put a record on."

This made my blood boil and prompted me to threaten him with violence if he ever insulted my roommate again. He never did. *Result!*

This only goes to show that even among people with disabilities, a certain amount of piss taking goes on.

But there has been a huge shift in public attitudes towards disability and the Paralympic athletes have played a significant role in affecting that positive change. There are now more people with disabilities on TV, like Alex Brooker who co-hosts Channel 4's topical comedy series The Last Leg.

He was born with missing fingers on both hands and wears a prosthetic leg after his right one had to be amputated when he was a baby.

The Last Leg tackles the subject of disability in a refreshingly non patronising way that doesn't alienate able bodied viewers, it is rather patchy as a comedy show with some material falling short of the mark.

But, that said, to have the issue talked about on prime time TV is a major step forward. The Last Leg isn't exclusively about disability though and can have a real topical bite. Donald Trump, the most dangerous and embarrassing US President ever, was a popular and, let's face it, easy target.

We also have 'The A-Word' on the BBC which focuses on autism and the excellent TV drama There She Goes which is also on the Beeb and features a couple struggling to raise a daughter with a severe learning disability.

There's also a presenter on Countryfile who is a wheelchair user, and an actress who recently appeared on CBeebies who also happened to have part of her arm missing. She read a bedtime story on the channel and this actually prompted one parent to complain to the BBC that the fact she was missing part of her arm would give her child nightmares. Really? Just remind me, which century are we living in again?

I still believe people with disabilities are still at the bottom of the heap when it comes to employment and big charities like Scope could set a far better example when it comes to giving us paid jobs.

Scope, the national charity for people with cerebral palsy, finally appointed the first disabled Editor of its magazine in 2007, when former BBC man Ian Macrae took up the post.

About time, I say.

One reason why I went to university was to give me better chance of a job I actually wanted when I left.

When The Spastics Society changed its name to Scope, I breathed a huge sigh of relief, vainly hoping that the word 'spastic', that ugly, bastardised word that had been the bane of my life, would disappear from our vocabulary altogether.

But this large and wealthy organisation's record on issues like disability employment is poor, with only 18% of employees who took part in a recent in-house survey identifying themselves as living with some sort of impairment.

According to the Office for National Statistics – ONS – 4.1m of the UK's 7.7m disabled people are currently in work.

While our Paralympic athletes have played a part in affecting positive change, I identify far more closely with the late Irish painter and writer Christy Brown, whose story inspired the Oscar-winning movie, My Left Foot. My disability is similar to his, while not being so severe.

Other disabilities are available.

I even look a bit like Christy, especially around the eyes.

Speaking as someone who, when growing up, could be verbally abused up to eight times a week, I actually believed we were living in more enlightened times when it came to disability.

But the comedian and writer Rosie Jones, who has written material for the likes of Harry Hill appeared on Question Time recently and was asked about the impact of the Disability Discrimination Act on the lives of the people it was introduced to help.

Jones, who has cerebral palsy, said while progress had been made, she said disabled people are still at the bottom of the social heap when it comes to things like employment.

That's hardly surprising really because the agencies set up to help people like me into work are, in general, fucking useless.

One woman I saw, who I won't name, was lovely and we got on like the proverbial house on fire. There was one occasion when we collapsed into a fit of hysterics at the end of one of our meetings at the job centre and this burst of laughter attracted the attention of one of the security staff who came over to our desk to see if everything was alright. In his defence, laughter is probably not heard that often inside the walls of a job centre, is it?

I saw this woman for several months and all she managed to do for me was get me on Linkedin. There was also the occasion when I travelled all the way into Manchester to see someone from another 'employment agency' only to be told she was off sick. While I do have a temper like everyone else, I can generally keep it in check and resisted the temptation to drop a few f bombs!

But Jones, who has become a regular on several TV shows in recent months, did say something which did make me raise an eyebrow because I thought we were living in more enlightened times. She said whenever she goes out alone, she has to wear headphones in order to block out abuse from people in the street.

While these incidents tended to happen largely at night, with groups of people laughing and commenting about how drunk she looks and so on, they are now taking place more often during the day.

The same thing happened to me when I was walking through Manchester city centre recently after going to see a play at the Royal Exchange and a homeless man screamed at me that I shouldn't drink so much. The chance would be a fine thing! While this felt like an unwelcome blast from the past, I dismissed his outburst because he was obviously three sheets to the wind himself.

I was waiting for a cab at Altrincham taxi rank recently with a guy who, it transpired, was waiting to meet a friend. The friend turned up, nodded in my direction and said: "I see you've got a mate." The guy just laughed and said "Yeah – he reminds me of you." I assume these were veiled references to my disability and I was seconds away from calling out both ignoramuses. As in the bad old days, I just clammed up and didn't say a word.

I knew exactly what I wanted to say – the words stuck in my mouth. This was how it was in the bad old days. Back then, the more upset I got the more unintelligible my speech became and besides it did prevent these situations escalating into a punch up, which I would have lost. While I'm strong, even stronger after being a member of a gym for more than 10 years, I'm not quick enough when it comes to landin a decisive punch.

Those two incidents sound oh so trivial when compared to the issues highlighted in the BBC documentary Targeted: The Truth About Disability Hate Crime. Screened in January 2021, programme featured a string of horrific stories about the way in which several disabled people had been verbally and physically abused over the years.

The victims of hate crime included a lady from Northern Ireland who had been hounded out of her home by neighbours who mistakenly thought she was getting special treatment from the welfare state and another woman who was blind and had been repeatedly mugged and had her guide dog kicked in the street.

There was one guy who was beaten up by a gang of yobs at a bus stop for no apparent reason other than that he was autistic.

The programme was a very, very difficult watch because those behind these hate crimes are wrecking the lives of disabled people.

If I had my way, they would be named and shamed and given hefty fines. If they didn't change their appalling behaviour, they should go to prison.

Being the subject of verbal abuse has undoubtedly had a lasting effect on me because it has damaged my self-esteem and has also made it difficult for me to make friends because it takes a long time for me to trust people.

While I would never dream of verbally abusing anybody – not even Man United fans – I've often wondered how much of a role fear plays in the mind set of those who carry it out.

There are certain disabilities that used to strike fear into me, like blindness for example.

I used to think of blindness as being the worst disability in the world. But I soon realised after I became a reporter how people with visual impairments can lead full and fulfilling lives. People like Mike Newman, who I had the pleasure of interviewing several times when I was at the Messenger.

His numerous achievements included breaking the UK blind land speed record by reaching a speed in excess of 140mph.

Then there was a brilliant blind pianist called Denis Friedman who I came across purely by chance in the bar next to Manchester's Palace Theatre. I'd called in for a quick pint on my way home and I remember how mesmerised I was as we the audience watched him play, his fingers dancing effortlessly from one end of the keyboard to the other.

Denis used to live in Stretford, one of the areas covered by the Messenger and this meant I could interview him.

Without wishing to sound like I'm bragging, I guess I've achieved an awful lot, really. I often wax lyrical like a sentimental old fool about the three years I spent at Sheffield University. There's no doubting it was the passport to a brilliant social life, with me rarely going to bed before 4am at weekends.

But my main reason for upping sticks to South Yorkshire was it would also be a stepping stone to a good job.

Me and my friends really enjoyed everything student Sheffield had to offer from pubs and trips to the dirt-cheap union bar to the weekly disco at the Octagon Centre, where you could play the popular game of trying to dance in a sea of spilt lager.

Then there were the gigs. I've always enjoyed live music even though the artists performing might not produce the sort of music I'm into.

While I was at university, we music fans were spoilt rotten and I was lucky enough to see top acts like The Damned, Tom Robinson, The Pogues, New Order and Billy Bragg.

The Pogues were so drunk by the time they staggered on stage at the Octagon – a multi-purpose venue next to the student union – it was a miracle they could still stand up. However, that didn't stop them putting in a performance that was riotously memorable as they brought the house down.

We even found time for some studying!

But the winters in Sheffield were cold. Bitterly cold.

For instance, when I went to lectures, I would wear a jumper, a bomber jacket, my overcoat, gloves and a hat and even with all those layers on, I was just about warm enough.

It wasn't uncommon for the temperature to remain below freezing day and night for *three months*. I can even remember foot long icicles hanging down from the porch of my student house.

On one occasion the lock on our front door froze and this winter wonderland seemed a world away from the sprinkling of the white stuff we usually get back in Greater Manchester.

But at least the pub was nice and warm.

My student house was a rambling, dry stone affair that looked like something the Adams Family would live in.

The only form of heating was the cooker in the kitchen, and I was given the room that had the boiler in it, on the grounds it would be the warmest and I can remember with a shudder coming back after the Christmas holiday to find ice on the *inside* of my bedroom window.

That was a whole new experience for me – and not one I would ever care to repeat.

I shared the place with six born again Christians including a very strange girl who kept pet rats in a cage on the phone table. These 'adorable' creatures used to shit outside the back of the cage. Thankfully, cleaning up their mess was the sole preserve of their owner.

Rats and snakes are the only animals I'm genuinely scared of. I've been terrified of rats ever since I watched the film version of Orwell's novel 1984. I refer to the infamous scene with the rats in which Winston Smith comes within seconds of having a group of the horrid creatures gnaw at his face.

I reviewed a stage version of this chilling tale at The Lowry and during the infamous scene with the rats, the theatre company decide to gradually increase the volume of the sound effect they were using so it actually felt like they were moving around under the theatre seats.

I was also once given the chance to hold a snake which is another of God's creatures, I'm absolutely terrified of even though I'm acutely aware there aren't any poisonous ones in this country. With a palpable shudder I politely declined the invitation.

Sharing a house at university with people who aren't related to you is a great learning curve. It was the first time I had to think about things like paying bills or doing a food shop. Previously, those things had been something my mum and dad did for me.

It still makes me smile when I think of the time me and Tim – the only other lad in the house – brewed some beer. Tim was very rarely in Sheffield at the weekends because he went back to Manchester to see his girlfriend.

So, me and James, who was going out with one of the girls in our house, decided to have a tasting session which saw us drink most of the booze Tim and I had made. Naughty, naughty!

When I lived in my student house, I was mad about one of my housemates and got to spend a lot of time with her. I thought she was gorgeous and used to pretend in my head we were going out together.

I even thought I had a vague chance of turning a close friend into an actual girlfriend because she wasn't always in a relationship. But guess what, even when she was single, she wasn't fucking interested.

Her loveliness extended beyond her looks, and she was a really good listener. She was someone you could take your problems to and be guaranteed a sympathetic ear.

Going to university is a great learning curve – in more ways than one. It was while studying in Sheffield that I tried my first ever joint and while I would never encourage anyone to smoke pot, I found the experience a very enjoyable one. Especially because since adolescence and my secondary dystonia rearing its ugly head, relaxing was very difficult for me.

But please bear in mind, the hash we smoked was nowhere near the strength of what you can buy today.

However, after first year I quietly resented my group of friends after they excluded me when they made arrangements to live out in second year. While we continued to meet socially now and again, I spent a lot of my weekends with Karen and Mary, two great girls from my English course who were like a comedy act and my future housemate, who I quietly loved.

We took my son James to see my old haunts and the trip wouldn't have been complete without a trip to see my former student digs. The house has since been transformed into what now looks like a habitable family home. But I resisted the temptation to knock at the front door and ask for a quick tour for old time's sake. I was scared the current owner might think I was a loony and call the police!

But when you go back somewhere you can't *really* go back. You're older, if not necessarily wiser, and the people you had your fun with aren't there anymore. Or to put it another way, the dynamic has changed.

Anyway, back to my work experience.

The summer of 1983 was baking hot – so much so we had water fights in our lunch hour at college and the weather was so warm our clothes would be dry again by the time our lunch break was over. It was the first inclination that our climate was changing with temperatures passing 80 degrees.

I spent a week at the Messenger, a publication at the heart of the community it served. It was founded by Eddy Shah in the 1970s.

The banter in the office was great and everyone was so welcoming I felt like part of the furniture after just a couple of days. I also found a kindred spirit in chief reporter Steve Hammond, who shared the same politics as me. We also had a very similar sense of humour.

The Messenger has always been politically neutral. But Steve and I most definitely weren't and in between writing stories we spent time putting the world to rights. I found that pretty easy because I hated Margaret Thatcher and everything our then Prime Minister stood for. Her infamous statement about there being 'no such thing as society' sends a chill down my spine even to this day.

My political views had been shaped by watching Alan Bleasdale's seminal TV drama, Boys from the Blackstuff. Interviewing my hero was a high-water mark in my career as a journalist and when I told him his work had shaped my politics and he said "Good." The interview was the writer's only print interview in the noughties and I did it to mark the 25th anniversary of the acclaimed drama's original release. It was a major triumph for me.

It was while watching Blackstuff that I first became socially and politically aware. For the uninitiated, it followed a group of labourers in Liverpool in the 1980's, when job prospects for millions of people were unbelievably grim.

Having grown up in safe, suburban Sale I previously had only a limited knowledge as to how Thatcher's policies were devastating the lives of millions of working people and I found it deeply, deeply disturbing.

For me, the best episode was Yosser's Story starring Bernard Hill in the title role. Hill memorably plays a mentally ill man who has been left to fend for himself in a society that has seemingly lost its ability to care.

Now I challenge anybody not to be moved by this, as we watch a man whose already lost his job and his sanity, running the risk of losing his three kids into the bargain.

I don't think I've ever seen a TV drama that affected me as deeply as Boys from the Blackstuff did.

After receiving a copy of the article in the post, Alan even sent me a postcard thanking me for a 'thoughtful piece.'

My mum had it put in a double-sided block glass frame which now has pride of place in my living room.

I often wondered why a writer who once was so prolific in the 80's and 90's went so quiet. Many of the social issues he championed haven't gone away.

We have food banks in 21st century Britain, for God's sake.

Alan Bleasdale made a comeback of sorts with The Sinking of the Laconia on Channel 4 in 2016. It was an absorbing tale about a German U-boat captain who, during the Second World War, ordered the sinking of a ship he believed was carrying Allied troops and weapons.

When the captain became aware that he'd been given duff intelligence he tried to do the right thing. He bought his U-boat to the surface and started to rescue the passengers, the majority of which turned out to be civilians.

The Sinking of the Laconia was watchable rather than memorable and while the horror of the events on which it's based had only a limited emotional impact on me when I watched it, failed to care what happened to the characters. Bleasdale is a writer who is at his best when writing about social issues like poverty and unemployment.

My son James, now 21, sat through an episode of GBH with me one day and said it was "really good."

This leads me to the conclusion there's a timeless quality to his work and a Bleasdale revival is long overdue on TV.

The Channel 4 series starred Robert Lindsay as the power mad council leader Michael Murray, in what is still for me one of the finest performances of a long and distinguished career.

Murray, who has evidently been emotionally damaged by a troubled childhood, rules an unnamed northern city like a latter-day Adolf Hitler, crushing dissent and surrounding himself with 'yes men' and hired thugs.

According to its writer, GBH wasn't a veiled attack on the former leader of Liverpool City Council, Derek Hatton. Murray is a far more interesting character than the colourful and controversial politician, he said.

Another writer from Merseyside, Jimmy McGovern, is undoubtedly the heir to Bleasdale in terms of the way he gives a voice to the voiceless.

While there's nothing wrong with the frilly romantic period pieces in which pampered ladies get their petticoats in a twist wondering what to wear for an up-and-coming ball, TV drama is at its best, for me anyway, when it challenges us the viewers and makes us sit up and think.

McGovern's play about the Hillsborough football disaster in 1989 in which 97 football fans needlessly lost their lives was particularly pertinent to me. I went to university with two of the people who died in this horrific disaster, Rick Jones and Tracey Cox. Tracey introduced me to what became my group of friends and Rick looked out for me as I initially struggled to get used to student life.

I never had the chance of meeting Jimmy McGovern and interviewing him. Which is a pity.

I did my work experience on the trusty electric typewriter I used at school and later at Loreto Sixth Form College in Hulme, Manchester. I started there after the Moss Side riots, in September 1981. Now I know the Catholic Church received much criticism in recent years for past misdemeanours, but I was in their education system until the age of 19 and they couldn't have been any more caring or supportive to me.

This support even extended to the college Principal Sister Magdalene taking me home with her so I could finish one of my exams. It was a sweltering early summer day and almost everyone else had gone home and I hadn't finished my paper.

With a temperature that was more like Majorca rather than central Manchester, Sister M even mopped my brow to cool me down. I'd always had extra time so I could complete them, and the college was about to close that day, so it seemed like the logical thing to do.

The nuns at Loreto were particularly inspirational, people like Sister Magdalene and Sister Margaret. But Father Merriman, who taught me Religious Studies O Level, was very odd. He was the only teacher I've ever had a clash of personalities with, and things got so bad one day I actually stormed out of the classroom. But he knew his stuff and I got a grade B in my O Level exam.

It was while I was at college, I had my first play performed, a short play called The Box. It was a piece about a prisoner who is haunted by figures from his past in a recurring nightmare. It featured a college friend of mine called Tom Reilly in the lead role – there wasn't any nepotism involved I hasten to add – and ended with the prisoner waking up and letting out an ear-piercing scream.

It opened with a few seconds of The Box, a suitably sinister song by the cult artist Fad Gadget, a haunting piece of music that in my view, perfectly set the tone. The song was chosen because I felt it reflected the sense of claustrophobia felt by a man haunted by his past as he languished in a prison cell.

My education began at Forest School in Timperley, near Altrincham. But I had to leave at the age of seven.

My parents decided to take me out because the school was unable to give me the one-to-one support I needed for Maths. The lessons took place at home and the powers that be made me go into school after lunch therefore I missed the morning lessons on the grounds that me arriving late in the morning would be too disruptive for the other kids. This meant I missed a sizeable chunk of the school day, so I left at the age of seven.

My memories of Forest are naturally dim now. I can remember going for tea at my pal Steven Goddard's house and falling in the pond in the family's garden. Steven to the rescue! He jumped in the water, wearing a face mask and a snorkel in a bid to pull me out.

He was a lovely lad who didn't have a bad bone in his body, and I was so sorry to hear he'd died. Rest in peace, Steve.

On a lighter note, I also remember bursting into tears after seeing one of my fellow pupils in a monster mask one Halloween, believing it to be real. I can laugh about it now, of course, but at the time it seemed very, very real.

Some of the other kids used to try to snaffle a piece of my chocolate biscuit at lunchtime, which was the closest I ever got to being bullied while at Forest.

Then I moved to All Saints in Sale – which was where I tasted academic failure for the first time in the shape of the 11 plus exam.

The 11 plus was for many kids a passport to a grammar school education. But the fact it contained so many Maths questions meant I had more chance of passing a test in Swahili. The teacher I had in the top class wasn't much help either. If he thought you could pass the 11 plus, he was metaphorically all over you but if you weren't, you might as well have been invisible.

While Maths has always been the bane of my life, miracles can happen, and I left my secondary school with a grade 2 pass in the old CSE exam. A grade 1 was the equivalent of a grade C at O Level, which came before what are now GCSEs. The miracle worker was Mrs Hoyle who gave me one-to-one support in a subject I loathe even to this day.

With her brown shoulder length hair and brown rimmed glasses, Mrs H looked like the Greek singer Nana Mouskouri, which was ironic really because she came from Burnley!

My best friend at All Saints was called Gary Craven who suffered the double ordeal of losing both his parents by the age of 10. Gary's personality changed, and we drifted apart. We even came to blows one day.

It was only years later I could empathise with him, the fact he'd been so cruelly deprived of his mum and dad at such a tender age. When he changed as a result of this double tragedy, he became aggressive towards me. I didn't appreciate what he was going through, and I just thought he was being difficult. Very selfish, I know. But I was only ten.

So naturally our friendship fizzled out.

But I am eternally grateful to the headmaster at All Saints for letting me have the one-to-one Maths tuition which I had to have at home while I was at Forest. Obviously, I can't say this definitely would have been the case, but had I not attended mainstream schools I doubt I would have achieved what I went on to achieve, both academically and professionally.

No amount of teaching could have prepared me for the amount of bullying and name calling that went on in the playground and I'm sure such attitudes wouldn't be tolerated today.

At the time, there were only a handful of BAME pupils in the whole school and I can remember one lad called Richard, being subjected to a catalogue of vile racist abuse. It was ironic we shared the same name as I too experienced name calling for the first time.

But it was the 70s.

This experience did, however, instil my lifelong affinity with the BAME community. I took comfort from the knowledge there is another group of people going through the same thing as me. Not because of a disability – because of the colour of their skin.

But I wouldn't dream of equating what I went through with what black people still have to endure today.

Nor have I ever had to endure violence because I'm disabled. The only violence I've suffered has always been verbal rather than physical.

I've never been verbally abused by a member of the BAME community because I'm sure they know exactly what it feels like.

Some of the punishments meted out to the pupils at All Saints just wouldn't be tolerated today. The slipper was still in use, and I can remember my teacher in the top class hitting me on the head with closed knuckles when he thought I'd been naughty.

But there were occasions when I *had* been naughty like the occasion when we were briefly left to our own devices in the top class and most of the lads instigated what can be described as a small-scale riot which ended with poor old Anthony Craig having a pair of trousers from lost property placed on his head and buttoned up!

Most of the miscreants involved got a couple of licks of the slipper as punishment for our bad behaviour. While my backside stung like hell afterwards, I was determined to play the tough guy and not let my classmates see me cry.

The most humiliating punishment was being made to stand on a chair in front of the whole class to explain why I'd missed Sunday Mass. Any explanation you came up with was instantly dismissed. It really felt like you were on trial. This particular punishment was later phased out at All Saints. What a way to put kids off religion – for life.

But it was the 70s.

When we left, we had to sing a medley of songs at the leaver's assembly. That was quite a challenge for someone who knows one note and that note is V flat. Unlike my dad and my brother Jon who relish being in the limelight, I absolutely hate it. I can even remember trying to hide at the back when we put on this leavers assembly concert only because I couldn't find a stone to crawl under!

In the unlikely event of me ever winning an award for anything I would be far happier sending someone else to collect it in my place. Unless the prize was being presented by the stunning French actress Joséphine Jobert. Then I'd force myself.

Blessed Thomas Holford in Altrincham, my secondary school, was much more enjoyable. This was thanks to Mr Smith – our headmaster – and his staff. I was still calling him 'Sir' and 'Mr Smith' when we spoke at a school reunion years later. I guess putting my hand up to ask if I could go to the loo was taking it too far, though.

Now for the biography bit.

The eldest of three children, I was born on January 26, 1965, at Southfields Maternity Home which was in Bowdon, then part of Cheshire. When asked to give my address I always put 'Cheshire' rather than 'Trafford' because it sounds nicer, somehow. A bit classier, too.

Southfields is now apartments and one recently went on the market for £585,000.

Famous people to share my birthday include the Hollywood legend Paul Newman, which is pretty cool.

A lad who went on to be a good mate of mine at secondary school was nicknamed 'Paul Newman' by my PE teacher. Presumably it was down to his pointy chin.

When I was at the Messenger some of the lads said I reminded them of the entertainer Gary Wilmot. Personally, I've always thought I look more like the 70's heartthrob Donny Osmond.

I was born on the same day they held Winston Churchill's funeral at Westminster Abbey. What a debt of gratitude we owe to that remarkable man and the entire wartime generation.

I'm the only one in the family to become a journalist. I'm also the only one of my siblings not to go to grammar school. But I did receive a top-class education at a caring and very supportive secondary school and got my first step on the academic ladder which eventually led to a career in newspapers. My brother Jon is a teacher and Carrie, my sister, works as a speech therapist in the picture postcard county of Herefordshire.

Between us we have five kids – I have a 21-year-old son called James who is a digital media student and Jon has his two stepdaughters, Amber and Grace. Carrie also has two girls, Sophie and Iz (Isabelle).

At the time of writing, James, a digital media student, is about to start a supported internship at MediaCity in Salford which has filled him with much excitement.

He's even spoken of becoming a journalist one day.

When he was 15, James did a week's work experience at the Messenger, which sort of felt like history repeating itself in a way.

He rounded off his week by writing an excellent film review.

They say the apple doesn't fall far from the tree, after all.

I really enjoyed my time at BTH, which, for some reason had been nicknamed the British Torture House by some of my fellow pupils. It was a deeply misleading nickname as there was nothing torturous about the place at all.

The teachers were kind and supportive, but you knew there was a line you shouldn't dare cross where discipline was concerned. When I was there the cane was the ultimate deterrent and one of the teachers used to strap your backside if you stepped out of line.

Luckily, I managed to escape both.

96 per cent of my fellow pupils didn't bother about me being different and treated me like one of them. In fact, you could say I became a bit of a celebrity. I always preferred hanging around with the so-called naughty kids as they were far more fun to be around and maybe this helped me to ingratiate myself with my peers.

My own flirtation with 'naughtiness' while at secondary school didn't extend beyond thundering around the school with my electric typewriter on a trolley, fellow pupils scattering in my path. Although I did sneak the occasional cig on my way to school, which was quite daring/foolish when you consider my woeful lack of dexterity.

I always found the 'naughty kids' far better company and far more fun than the goody two shoes set. When some of the kids sneaked a fag behind the bike sheds, I was always the lookout.

My sense of humour, which can be crude and childish to this day, also helped when it came to ingratiating myself with my classmates. I was more than happy to play the class clown.

But as Shakespeare once said – all the world's a stage and all the men and women merely players.

The only year I didn't like at secondary school was the third year when I was forced to move forms because my own class did all their lessons upstairs. It was impossible to get my typewriter upstairs on its trolley, so I found myself temporarily studying with a group of people I barely knew and, to be honest, didn't like much.

Also, they all seemed to know each other and were in their own little cliques which made me feel like the proverbial fish out of water.

So, I had to meet my mates at lunch time only. Which I hated.

I was at BTH for five years and escaped with just one detention after being wrongly accused of spitting out my chewing gum and it landing in another lad's hair. He was a real pain in the arse. But I would never have done him any harm. He reminded me of Perfect Peter from the Horrid Henry books. But even more nauseating.

The teacher who 'saw' what happened even told me Simon had to have a piece of hair cut out so the gum could be removed.

I carried on protesting my innocence and the teacher obviously thought I protested too much because it was detention at the double for me.

Why this teacher didn't believe me remains a mystery to this day. She even roped in a colleague in a bid to ratchet up the guilt factor. But I had nothing to be guilty of.

Maybe they just didn't like me.

The first session of detention was actually grist to the mill for me because me and my fellow detainees were told by the teacher that we had to write a short story on any subject we wanted to.

But teachers aren't daft and the next time we were told to write about a subject that was more obscure.

It was while at secondary school that I had my first crush – in the shape of a gorgeous fifth former called Julie Kane. She was lovely. But Julie was in the top class, and I was a snotty nosed 12-year-old. Then there was Donna, another fifth former, who seemed fixated on this stick insect of a lad from my year.

When I showed an interest in Donna her best mate said to me "You've not got much of a physique, have you?" – a statement I found laughable rather than hurtful.

Sadly, the lovely Julie turned out to be the first in a very long line of unrequited crushes. Over the years I've met scores of girls and women who were more than willing to be my friend. But none who were willing to take things further.

But I did have a minor snogging session with a girl from school who came to my 12th birthday party. She was called Hannah – not her real name – but the snogging session didn't lead anywhere.

I carried on liking Hannah throughout secondary school and can remember crossing out her boyfriend's name a few times when I saw she'd scrawled it on a piece paper in a teacher's office. I was very jealous – big time.

I continue to find my lack of luck in love deeply frustrating – that much trotted out saying 'there's someone for everyone' just doesn't ring true for me and it never has. But I am toying with the idea of joining a dating agency at some point and that is one New Year resolution I intend to keep.

Many people think university is one big Roman orgy with 'those young people' who go forever engaged in constant bouts of partying and bed hopping. While the first part of that statement is definitely true, the bit about the bed hopping certainly wasn't true for me and my mates. A lot of the students tended to be in long term relationships either with people who were studying elsewhere or who'd opted to stay at home.

When I finally started going out with someone at the ripe old age of 26, I found a lot of able-bodied women were more relaxed around me, presumably because they knew I wasn't likely to make a play for them.

But I'd never stopped being a 'normal male' in terms of my sex drive and I had no outlet for these desires for many, many years.

Consequently, I was very jealous of Mark Todd – who you'll meet later in the book – for having an able-bodied girlfriend. Please, please don't get me wrong. Having a partner with a disability isn't second best. Depending on the disability of course, it can cause problems when two disabled people get together, particularly with the physical side of things.

I don't want to paint myself as some sort of sex addict. But I do think there has to be a certain amount of physical attraction in a relationship for it to work. It would just be nice to have someone who shared my interests and not just on a purely platonic level.

While I was at Sheffield, I resigned myself to the fact that the chances of me finally meeting a partner were as remote as they had always been, so I just concentrated on having good time and have a good time I certainly did. I never realised socialising could be so cheap. A pint of lager in the student union cost less than 70p. So, what was not to like?

All students should make the most of their time at university because before you know it, it's over.

But there is some work to be done too, like having to read 23 Shakespeare plays in second year. It was while I was at Sheffield that I fell in love with the poetry of William Blake. Deceptively simple, they're also open to a variety of interpretations.

As for Shakespeare, I initially found Hamlet and The Tempest a bit of a slog when I studied them for A level. But one day it just all fell into place and Hamlet is for me the best play ever written, period.

But it was while I was at BTH that I saw my name in print for the first time. I had a couple of poems published in the school magazine. It gave me a real sense of satisfaction and an appetite for more.

My best mate for most of my time there was John Ryder, a huge lad whose dad had been left disabled after he'd had a stroke. I can remember me and Andy Wallis, who also hung around with us, having a crush on John's very glamorous sister Christine, who we thought looked a bit like Hollywood star Farah Fawcett Majors. Her broad Manchester accent just didn't suit her at all.

But maybe John and I became pals because we were united by the same thing – disability. He had a natural empathy towards me after what happened to his dad, also called John, who had been a very successful businessman before he became ill.

John and Ellen Ryder, John's mam and dad, were 'salt of the earth' as we say in these parts. They are no longer with us.

I remember them coming to Lourdes with me, my mum and brother in 1984 and seeing an improvement in John's condition. Lourdes is a place in France where the Virgin Mary is supposed to have appeared to Saint Bernadette and a shrine has been made where the sighting took place.

I went to Lourdes a cynical 19-year-old but it's probably the only time in my life I've actually found inner peace. The premise behind this place is that the sick go there to be healed and it's quite a sight, seeing the sticks and crutches discarded by those who claim they no longer needed them.

My first best mate at secondary school was also called John – maybe I just gravitated towards people of that name.

As I was about to leave BTH my parents came up with the idea of having a shield named after me. It was dubbed The Richard Bowen Award for Special Effort. The award is presented to pupils who achieve success against the odds.

Funnily enough, I never thought of what I was doing as 'special' and I was taken aback when Mr Rhodes, my PE teacher turned to me after a class one day and said: "You've got guts, lad." Who, me?

Mr Rhodes treated my various physical challenges with unwavering and engaging good humour. He also made me 'man up' and I can remember tripping on the cinder football pitch at school, splitting my knee open and refusing medical treatment until we'd finished the game. It was a bit like when England defender Terry Butcher playing on with that head wound for England in the 1990 World Cup semi-final. Except I didn't have a bandage on.

Well, maybe that is stretching things a bit.

I left secondary school after five happy years in 1981 and I hope I paved the way for other kids with disabilities to come after me. The very thought of being a trail blazer gives me a real sense of satisfaction.

Like the vast majority my peers, I had no idea what I wanted to do as a job when I left. But there was one job I that was definitely off the table. Dancer.

While at BTH we had a couple of lessons in country dancing, and I certainly made a big impression. Unfortunately, it was on the feet of the poor girl who ended up being my partner

I was the John Sergeant of my year – but without his sense of timing!

Most of the kids who took part in the dance class hated it as much as I did and if memory serves it was never repeated again. Thank goodness!

When I was working at The Messenger years later, I was fortunate enough to review some world class dancing when the Kirov and the Bolshoi Ballet respectively came to The Lowry. Until then I'd never fully realised the level of grace and beauty and poise attainable by the human body.

It was an evening of dance I'll never forget and along with a couple of thousand others I floated my way out of the auditorium on my way home. It was life affirming stuff.

And I wasn't even a ballet fan!

The first story I wrote while on work experience at the Messenger was about a fire in Trafford Park, the huge industrial estate on the outskirts of the borough. Steve the chief reporter took me in his car, and I wrote the piece up when we returned to Sale, just like a real reporter.

I seemed to make a good impression while I was at the SAM, which is more than can be said for one memorable character who used our newly installed access to the Internet to search out some hard-core porn during his lunch break. I guess you could call it research – of a different kind. The sort of material he found left nothing to the imagination and I never saw him again after that. He didn't think to delete his search history. Oops!

When I first started at the paper as a staff reporter, we had two editions, covering Sale and Altrincham and Stretford and Urmston. Two editions have since become one and the Messenger is now produced from an office in Bolton.

It covers an area called Trafford south of Manchester which was born out of local government reorganisation in 1974. Previously, the borough had been divided into Cheshire and Lancashire, respectively.

The borough fertile ground for a journalist and you're never short of interesting things to write about.

As far as I can remember, there's always been a Conservative MP in the south of the borough and while our politics couldn't be further apart, I have a great deal of respect and admiration for the current holder of the Altrincham and Sale West seat Sir Graham Brady, who I interviewed many, many times, for being an excellent constituency MP.

Graham is not blindly partisan and when I interviewed him at his home in Altrincham, he really surprised me by saying Tony Benn is one of the MPs he admires for being an outstanding Parliamentarian. Even though they're on completely opposite sides of the political fence.

He succeeded Sir Fergus Montgomery.

The main towns that make up Trafford are Sale, Altrincham, Stretford and Urmston, Davyhulme, Old Trafford and their surrounding districts.

Sale, where I grew up, was the birthplace of a number of famous people, including the playwright Robert Bolt whose writing credits include Dr Zhivago and A Man For All Seasons. Both of these later became classic films.

I covered the opening of the theatre that bears his name when it opened and had the pleasure of interviewing his widow, the actress Sarah Miles, who was special guest at the event.

A blue plaque now sits above Bolt's birthplace, now a business, on nearby Marsland Road. The theatre is part of the Waterside Arts Centre, an intimate and welcoming venue that also includes two art galleries and a café area.

The venue had been a long time in opening – I can remember writing my first story on the proposal for an arts centre for Trafford shortly after I joined the Messenger in 1992. Possible locations that were previously considered included the rather imposing old Victorian police station in Altrincham. It's a building with bags of character. But it never struck me as the most welcoming of buildings.

The Waterside used to be a dump of a place called Sale Civic Theatre, a monument to neglect.

However, it was here that I saw one of the best productions I've seen on the professional stage.

It was produced by a Trafford based company called Tranter Theatre who had set Strindberg's classic Miss Julie in South Africa when the country was in the grip of the appalling apartheid regime. The original play is the captivating tale of what happens when the social divide is crossed, and Tranter's production introduced a racial element to the story.

Famous names to have appeared at the Waterside, include Midge Ure former lead singer of the electro pop act, Ultravox. When I interviewed him, Midge told me his stage name is basically his real name, which is Jim, spelt backwards. Part of me thought it could be an 'in joke' about the flying insects for which his native Scotland is famous.

Speaking to Midge was a surreal experience, for it was he who helped organise Live Aid with Sir Bob Geldolf.

I always found that a challenge – trying to encapsulate the career of some celebrities in a 15-20-minute time slot. That was the amount of time we journalists were invariably allocated by their publicity officers. Talking to this friendly and accommodating Scot about Live Aid alone could certainly take up that time, and then some.

Other famous faces to grace this stage in Sale include Hugh Cornwell of The Stranglers. When I asked him how long we had for the interview he gave me the exact number of minutes and seconds, which was decidedly odd.

The newsreader John Suchet came to Trafford to share his love of classical music. While he waxed lyrical about the work of the great composers it has to be a song by Manchester indie giants The Smiths that best sums him up. This Charming Man. He also really appreciated me telling him how he used to come across as caring deeply about what he was reading when he was reading the news.

I've always been a massive fan of former Bake Off host Sue Perkins who brought her one woman show, The Really Disappointing Second Show, to the Waterside in 2007. What you see is what you get with this multi-talented comedian and presenter who is as likeable in real life as she is on stage or TV. She's witty, charming and has an easy manner. I'd even venture to guess she could even make the king of the curmudgeons crack a smile.

The show focussed on how life has a habit of letting us down and featured a 98-year-old homophobic grandmother. Unfortunately, I couldn't make it which was a pity as I couldn't think of a better way to spend an evening in the company of a woman who would surely make the perfect dinner guest. Even at the end of a phone, Sue's great fun.

She's also someone I'd like to be stuck on a desert island with because of the way she'd keep my spirits up.

The veteran actor Peter Sallis brought his one man show to the WAC in 2008. Despite a career spanning several decades, which saw him perform alongside acting royalty like Sir Laurence Olivier and Dame Judi Dench, he'll probably always be the voice of the hapless inventor Wallace in the Wallace and Gromit films.

But Sallis, who sounded every inch the ac-tor, was more than happy that these modern day classics with their quintessentially British humour, had introduced him to a whole new generation of young fans.

When it came to the success of the Wallace and Gromit films, Peter said it was largely down to their lead characters including the wonderful facial expressions worn by Gromit, who turned exasperation into an art form as his master's canine sidekick.

Another comedy with which the actor will forever be inextricably linked is the gentle BBC sitcom Last of the Summer Wine in which he played Clegg, the sensible one, in a much-loved show about three old men refusing to act their age.

The programme was tailor made for Sunday nights and Peter said its stars got on famously in real life too, which surely contributed to their on-screen chemistry. There was never a cross word spoken on set, apparently.

Sale was also the birthplace of one George Mottershead, the First World War veteran who founded Chester Zoo after he suffered life changing injuries in the trenches and was a wheelchair user for the rest of his life.

The town is also the birthplace of the radio presenter James H Reeve who is for me one of the most talented broadcasters ever to sit in front of a microphone. His style of broadcasting, when he fronted the late-night phone-in on Piccadilly Radio, was addictively confrontational. He was loosely comparable to the American style 'shock jock', winding up certain listeners with sublime skill.

But there's another of Sale's famous sons who can truly be described as a unique talent and who I regret never having had the chance to interview. Karl Pilkington is probably most famous for the travel series on Sky 1 called An Idiot Abroad in which he travelled the globe taking a sideways look at some of its most spectacular sights and tourist destinations including the Great Wall of China.

Sandy Wilson, who wrote the musical The Boyfriend, was also born in Sale.

People who break the mould and fly in the face of convention have always been a constant source of fascination for me as both a human being and as a journalist.

When I was freelancing, I interviewed an actor called Nabil Shaban for the newsletter producer by the disability arts organisation, North West Shape.

Shaban has brittle bones and uses a wheelchair. Back in those days – we met at the tail end of the 1980s - people with disabilities were part of an invisible population in our society and were rarely seen on a theatre stage. I met Shaban when he was about to play Hamlet at Manchester's old Green Room. He was wielding a sword at the time joked: "Don't worry – the worst it can do is poke your eye out."

The premise of the production, produced by the disabled people's theatre company Greae, was that Hamlet was stopped from being King because he was disabled. The original premise of the play is Hamlet has had the throne stolen from him by Claudius who has also married Hamlet's mother, Gertrude.

Altrincham, its neighbour three miles up the road, was the birthplace of the late war hero Bill Speakman who won the VC, the highest award for valour given to those serving in the military, for storming an enemy outpost single handed during the Korean War. During my interview he laid to rest forever the myth he used beer bottles during the attack after running out of ammunition. "Where would I get beer bottles from," he asked, with an expression of total bafflement written on his face.

Then there was the late comedian Chris Sievey, who came from Timperley, just outside Altrincham. For many years, he played a cult comedy character called Frank Sidebottom, complete with a large papier-mâché head and an unmistakable nasal twang. I got the chance to interview Sievey in character and it remains one of the most bizarre experiences in my career.

While his unique brand of humour didn't really chime with me, I always admire anyone who dares to be different and, as the lovable Frank, a throwback to the days of childhood innocence, he certainly was that.

Before he slipped on his now famous mask to become Frank, Sievey was lead singer of 70's punk band The Freshies. Punk passed me by – my musical tastes as I went into my early teens were embarrassingly safe and mainstream.

At the age of 13 I was a huge fan of The Bee Gees and pined for the day I'd be able to grow a hairy chest. These days, when chest fur is no longer fashionable, I jump at every opportunity I get to wax it off. But I never sank so low as to ask my parents for a medallion as a birthday present, like the one sported by Bee Gee Barry Gibb. That would have been so uncool.

Frank Sidebottom even inspired a movie called Frank and the leading character even wore his trademark papier-mâché head with the unmistakable goggle-eyes. The only difference being he wore it 24/7, to the point of even showering in it! I gave this particular flick, which featured Michael Fasbender in the title role, four stars for its kooky charm. But its creators insisted Frank, which was released in 2015, certainly wasn't a biopic.

If interviewing Sievey in character as Frank was the most bizarre experience of my career, there was a singer from Sale who turned up to the SAM office one day with his face totally obscured by bandages in the style of The Invisible Man.

That was *so* weird, especially when you consider the key role facial interaction plays during an interview. He'd aptly christened himself Mr X and after he'd left our receptionist joked that she was tempted to offer him a brew to see how he would drink it. Mr X's songs were dreadful, which is probably why he chose to hide his face!

I would love to know what happened to this decidedly off-the-wall character.

But there was another story I wrote that beat my interview with Frank hands down when it came to weirdness.

When the Body Worlds exhibition came to Manchester's Museum of Science and Industry I approached this job with a certain amount of trepidation because I'd heard the show featured real human cadavers preserved by the German anatomist Professor Gunter von Hagens.

Surely that couldn't be right, could it? That question kept flashing through my mind as I made my way to the MOSI.

But the rumours were right, and I was given one of the grisliest guided tours I've ever been on. The exhibition's creator had said this event would also give people an insight as to how certain lifestyle choices, like drinking and smoking, affect our insides.

Personally, I would rather look in a text book to get such information and my tour guide noted at the time: "I see you didn't hang around for long, Rick."

I 'hung around' long enough to get a feel of the show which went on to be a massive hit at the MOSI.

Then there was my experience with the colourful and controversial former MP George Galloway which taught me another valuable lesson in journalism – the ability to think on my feet. It was a Wednesday morning – the day when we finished the paper - and the phone rang in the Editor's office. "Rick – it's George Galloway," said Lynn, my Editor.

"What, *the* George Galloway," I asked. I'd expected his agent to call me back to confirm a date and time for the interview and while I'd done a small amount of research on this controversial character, I'd had no time to prepare some questions. So, my stress levels were going through the roof.

But I had a job to do. And I did it.

I have to say I really liked Galloway, who, despite his controversial views, I found to be a refreshing antidote to those bland politicians who are happy to tow the party line. Full of simmering Scottish passion, he was the type of bloke who could convince you black was white if you spent too long in his company.

It was hard to believe this very bright man had made the mistake of sidling up to Saddam Hussein as our country teetered on the brink of getting involved in the Gulf War had humiliated himself on national TV by pretending to be a cat in the Channel 4 reality show, Big Brother. He gave me the purr-fect interview.

While I worked hard to cultivate my own style of interviewing, there are other journalists I look up to.

My favourite interviewer has to be the unflinchingly forthright and unflappable Jeremy Paxman, former presenter of the BBC's Newsnight programme. Watching politicians of all complexions squirm as he gave them a relentless grilling was a great pleasure of mine.

But the politically neutral stance of the Messenger meant such grand inquisitions were not possible. Nor do I have Paxman's pushy personality.

Emma Barnett is also well worth a watch whenever she presents the programme for the way she also takes no nonsense from her interviewees.

Another great interviewer has to be Louis Theroux, whose laid-back manner conceals an uncanny ability to find out what makes people really tick. I've seen Theroux interview everyone from drug dealers to paedophiles in a disarmingly non-judgemental manner. I love Louis. He's one top journalist.

Learning to socialise wasn't easy for someone with a disability as obvious as mine. It took me a while to find my feet and find places where I felt at home. But find them I did.

I can remember for instance, going to a pub/disco called The Swinging Sporran in Manchester and coming very close to not being allowed in. The doorman never explained why – he just looked me up and down repeatedly. Maybe he thought I was pissed or on drugs or both.

But he eventually let me in after I convinced him I was there for somebody's birthday bash; somebody I knew from college. The place itself, no longer there now, was nothing more than a glorified dive and the doorman never explained the reason behind his reticent actions.

Then there was the time I went to meet someone in The Shakespeare pub in Manchester, arrived early and thought I'd get myself a pint while I was waiting. I asked the barmaid if she'd carry my beer to a table for me and you would have thought I'd just asked her for sex on the bar! But she eventually agreed, and I was able to quench my thirst.

But I eventually found places where I fitted in. My deep-seated love of music began in my late teens, so I thought I'd died and gone to heaven when The Hacienda, the coolest club I've ever been to, opened its doors in 1982.

I became a member in January 1983 and recall dancing to what was basically my record collection for two hours solid on student night. That must have annoyed the hell out of the club's owners who wanted us to spend our student cash over the bar.

The Hacienda was a place where my disability didn't matter because there were so many outlandish looking characters at the legendary club. This remarkable venue, which was years ahead of its time in terms of its layout and its lighting, stood on Whitworth Street West in the centre of Manchester.

It was also a place where people at the cutting edge of fashion could escape to its café for sausage and chips. I loved the contrariness of the place, and I loved its atmosphere even if the club was hardly packed to the rafters when I used to go.

The Hacienda changed its music policy when dance music largely took over the playlist and the music, I'd danced away the night to was suddenly replaced by a thudding, hypnotic beat.

In case you're wondering 'indie' is a term initially introduced to describe material released by the smaller, more independent record labels.

Equally enjoyable was joining the punks on the dance floor for a dance that involved everyone pushing one another in time to the music. That was so exhilarating, and it felt like I was part of some sort of bizarre cult.

My fellow dancers, sporting Mohicans so plastered in hair gel they were spiky enough to take your eye out, even toned down the mayhem whenever I danced near them. I never found out what this dance was called. But it was a fantastic way to release any pent-up teenage energy you had.

On one night I can actually remember a girl receiving a ticking off from her friend for staring at me. But the girl in question was looking at the clothes I was wearing, rather than staring at me because of my disability. I was wearing black trousers, black shirt, black overcoat and – wait for it – black leg warmers. It was a fashion faux pas that I was careful not to repeat.

The girl in question resisted the chance to take the piss. But my God, I deserved it!

The Has – as we rather unimaginatively nicknamed it – also helped launch the career of some artists who went on to become household names in pop. This included a certain Italian/American who became famous or should that be infamous for her raunchy stage persona. Her name is Madonna.

I also saw a couple of memorable gigs there featuring the unique musical talent who was Frank Tovey – aka Fad Gadget. You could describe his music as underground electronic, I guess. But he used the most unlikely things for percussion when he was in the studio – things like ashtrays and table legs. That may sound more than a little cracked. But it worked. The cult performer, who is no longer with us, wrote songs about subjects most artists just wouldn't touch, like the looming spectre of nuclear war.

Most people probably won't know who Fad Gadget was. But the chances are you'll have heard of one of the three ladies who formed his later backing group. Her name? Alison Moyet.

I have some really fond memories of that place and became very dewy eyed when my brother Jon bought me a black t-shirt bearing the Hacienda's distinctive logo. I also remember a very gentlemanly doorman who would clear the way for me whenever I wanted to leave the club early. Anyone at the front of the queue was unceremoniously pushed backwards – like I was a VIP trying to make a quick exit or something.

Dave Haslam was one of the DJs there and I had the pleasure of interviewing him in 2007, when he was hosting a show on the radio station, Xfm.

It felt like things had really come full circle in a way because I used to attend The Temperance Club, a night he hosted back in the day.

The Hacienda, a former yacht showroom, began life as an idea by Rob Gretton, the former manager of Joy Division and New Order. But most of the funding came from Tony Wilson, regarded by many as Mr Manchester, founder of the wonderful Factory Records.

Factory was so wonderful because it existed without following the conventions of the music business and I loved that as well as its unmistakable Mancunian identity.

Haslam described Wilson, who died of cancer in 2007, as someone who will never be replaced and said no one person will ever achieve what he did in his short lifetime.

That particular baton had, he insisted, been passed on to the bands, DJs and designers he inspired. Unfortunately, the closest I got to Tony Wilson was when I was in a room with him and some guests on Granada TV's late-night debate show, Upfront. This was a pity, as I think Tony Wilson would have made a fascinating interview and there's no doubting the massive impact, he had on the Manchester music scene.

I really enjoy listening to the radio and my favourite station has to be 6Music. The station's remit is to give a platform to new artists while, at the same time, never neglecting the classics produced by the giants of genres ranging from jazz to soul.

While working at the Messenger, I had the pleasure of interviewing two of the station's most well-known presenters in the shape of Mark Radcliffe and Marc Riley.

Riley used to be guitarist with the legendary Manchester band, The Fall. He currently presents the evening show, Monday to Thursday.

When we 'met' he was presenting the shows Rocket Science and Mint at the weekends.

For many years, he was one half of Mark and Lard, the double act which has since gone its separate ways. Marc played the role of Lard and was mercilessly ribbed for his size by Radcliffe.

The partnership was on Radio 1, and it was a partnership made in heaven for me. I loved the humour and their effortless camaraderie, something I've more recently found on The Sports Bar on Talksport.

Unfortunately, the duo who presented it have gone their separate ways and Andy Goldstein now presents the drive time show and his sidekick Jason Cundy now hosts The Sports Bar with Jamie O'Hara, three nights a week. I can still get my Goldstein/Cundy fix on Monday nights, the only night of the week they now work on the same show together.

They certain helped me get through the national lockdown last year at the height of the Coronavirus pandemic. They flit from serious to silly seamlessly and the phone-in attracts callers who are real characters, to put it mildly.

I listen a lot to the radio these days because most things on TV don't capture my imagination anymore. You also have to use your own imagination when listening to radio plays.

It was while working with the other Mark that Riley was able to interview pop legends like Sir Paul

McCartney. The broadcaster instantly warmed to Macca's affable and easy-going nature. Interviewing the established stars is an easy task for the simple reason that they have nothing to prove according to the former musician who was touring the world with The Fall while he was still in his teens.

Then there was their meeting with the legendary David Bowie whose huge back catalogue includes timeless classics like Starman, Ziggy Stardust and a song I would like to be played at my funeral, the rather wonderful Life On Mars.

Marc said he and Radcliffe experienced one or two butterflies as they waited to meet the pop icon in New York.

While they interviewed him it was hard to tell if Bowie was being serious or not, because he has one of those faces that gives nothing away and a very dry sense of humour to boot.

After leaving The Fall Marc formed his own band The Creepers, who stopped creeping in the late 80's.

One thing that's eminently likeable about Riley is his refusal to take himself too seriously when it comes to music, and I really like people like that.

The fact he's been there, done it and bought the t-shirt also allowed him a greater empathy with acts trying to make a name for themselves.

Most of the bands who appeared on Rocket Science were still searching for fame, after all.

Marc Riley who now presents a show on 6Music Monday to Thursday, reminds me of a music fan whose been let loose in a radio studio to play music he's passionate about.

The super cool Hacienda was a far cry from the disco I used to go to with a mate from school as a 13-year-old. It took place in a sports hall at Sale Leisure Centre, and it was crap. On our second visit we were the only people there.

We went on this sad excuse for a night out to try to meet girls and the only girl we ever saw was the one who stayed until the DJ had played a couple of Northern Soul tunes and then left. We only saw her once. She was also about 18-19 years old – far too old and far too cool for the likes of us. Even we got bored and quickly consigned this dreadful 'night out' to history.

It cost something like 20 or 30p to get in – even then we felt like we'd been robbed!

Socially I've never been that adventurous and prefer to 'play out' at places where I feel comfortable. One such place was The Wheatsheaf pub in Altrincham which was once a hive of activity, especially at the weekends when it was impossible to get a table after around 8.30pm. Its success was a result of the excellent people skills of Tommy and Linda Blease who made everyone feel welcome, especially me.

If there was such a thing as a Landlord and Landlady Factory it would have mass produced carbon copies of this lovely couple. After pulling their final pints at The Wheatsheaf they bought The Roebuck, a quaint and cosy little boozer with bags of character which is a 10-minute walk away. They invited me to follow them and I duly obliged. It was here that I had my 40th and 50th birthday parties respectively.

My next big birthday bash will be my 60th, which makes me feel very, very old.

Tommy and Linda gave me a place to go that was safe and idiot free. But I can count on one hand the number of disabled people I've seen socialising in pubs, bars, and restaurants over the years, despite improvements in terms of wheelchair access and so on.

The Wheatsheaf, once a magnet for so many young people, now stands empty and sad looking on Manchester Road in Altrincham.

An impressive looking building from the outside, it's surrounded by metallic fencing which makes me think it's only a matter of time before the developers moved in.

Music has always been a big part of my life and I've been lucky to attend some memorable gigs over the years – REM, Morrissey, David Bowie, The B-52s – to name just a few.

The area now known as Trafford has an impressive musical pedigree.

Altrincham is the birthplace of the singer Paul Young, not be confused with the purveyor of bland 80s pop ballads with a nice flattop hairstyle. This Paul Young was lead singer with the Manchester band Sad Café and also fronted Mike and the Mechanics later on in his career.

Altrincham Grammar School can also count Ian Brown and John Squire of legendary Manchester band The Stone Roses among its alumni.

Hale, which is just outside Altrincham, is also the birthplace of Peter Saville. He's designed record sleeves for numerous artists over the years including

Roxy Music, Joy Division, New Order and Orchestral Manoeuvres in the Dark

Saville certainly didn't come across as pretentious or remote like some creative types can be. But I guess when you're as talented as he is and you have produced a body of work like he has, there's no need to hide behind a façade.

Other famous musicians to come from the area include the tragic Ian Curtis, lead singer of 70's cult band, Joy Division. He was born in Old Trafford and raised in Macclesfield. For me, he's one of the greatest lyricists of all time and his lyrics, which are as poignant as they are profound are certainly comparable in terms of their emotional impact to the best contemporary poetry.

Fans of the teen love story Normal People which was shown on the BBC last year may well remember hearing a mellow, slower version of Love Will Tear Us Apart, Joy Division's final single.

A mural was unveiled to Curtis in Manchester city centre a few months ago and those eyes of his, full of intensity, give you the impression he's looking right through you. I often wonder what this most unlikely of geniuses would have gone on to become, had he lived. I also live a stone's throw from where the band played *that* legendary gig at Bowdon Vale Youth Club, just outside Altrincham, in March 1979.

Ian Curtis hanged himself in May 1980 on the eve of Joy Division's first American tour. He was taken from us far, far too soon.

There was one interview that evaded me while working at the SAM and it was a chat with Trafford's most famous musical export, Morrissey. The enigmatic lead singer of The Smiths was born in Davyhulme, near Stretford.

I've always been drawn to people who break the mould and 'Moz' definitely did that. Lanky and awkward looking with his NHS style specs, Morrissey somehow made awkwardness seem cool and he was also the first pop star to wax lyrical – no pun intended – about his love of literature. He adores Oscar Wilde.

Morrissey was such an intriguing character to me, and I even went as far as trying to dress like him. But I had to admit defeat when it came to his trademark quiff which for someone born with infuriatingly curly hair, was impossible to re-create.

I even went as far as plastering my barnet in blue hair gel which I bought from a hairdressing wholesaler in Sale.

The closest I got to Moz was an interview with his former bandmates, Mike Joyce and Andy Rourke. Joyce and Rourke were the drummer and bassist in The Smiths who I sadly never got to see live because tickets for the gigs were invariably snapped up within minutes and I could never get out of bed in time. They tended to go on sale at the weekends if memory serves me right.

What immediately struck me about Andy Rourke is how small he is. He's also from Sale and I later discovered we'd actually been to the same primary school. We met in the bar of Salford's Lowry Theatre, and I remember him being oh so impressed when I told him I owned every studio album The Smiths had ever made.

Any hope that the duo would say something revelatory about working with Morrissey were short lived as both musicians could only speak well of him.

I did get to interview Johnny Marr, The Smiths legendary guitarist and Morrissey's principal song writing partner actually, but it wasn't about musical matters. His niece attended Brentwood School in Timperley and Trafford Council has stirred up controversy when it decided to withdraw transport for students over the age of 16. The school meets the educational needs of young people with a range of disabilities and while there's no doubting the worthiness of the cause I also wanted to know what life had been like working in a band fronted by the most unlikely of pop stars.

Marr came across as polite and passionate when it came to rectifying what he thought was an obvious social wrong and the story has a happy ending, with the local authority eventually overturning its plans.

Martin Fry, lead singer of ABC, famed for their gold lame suits, is another famous musical export, hailing from Stretford.

I had the pleasure of interviewing Fry and while I never liked his band's music, it was impossible not to like this chatty man.

We also had something in common, in that we both studied English Literature at Sheffield University. One of his tutors also taught me and we reminisced about our trips to the Arts Tower where our lectures were held.

We used to go to the lecture hall in something called a paternoster lift, which had no front to it and required us students to jump into it when it reached our floor, making us feel like we were dicing with death as these lifts moved continuously between floors.

Fry got the joke and found my piece of 'lift nostalgia' very funny.

The 20-floor facility was demolished in 2013, after it was closed four years earlier. It was regarded as something of an architectural wonder in its day and was opened by Her Majesty The Queen Mother, in 1966.

Other famous people to hail from Trafford also include the actress Lynda Barron who comes from Urmston. She's probably most famous for playing nurse Gladys in the BBC sitcom Open All Hours, opposite Ronnie Barker.

I tried and tried to get an interview with Baron when I was working at the Messenger. But either she or her agent didn't seem interested and so I gave up in the end, which is more that can be said for Ronnie Barker's character in Open All Hours, who never stopped holding a torch for nurse Gladys.

Famous for his paintings depicting the hustle and bustle of life in working class Salford, the celebrated artist LS Lowry was actually born in Stretford, then a part of Lancashire. He may be most famous for his street scenes depicting a Salford that now only exists in the history books.

But Lowry was also a highly accomplished portrait painter and I enjoy these paintings an awful lot more.

They are currently on display at the arts centre in Salford that bears his name. The Lowry opened in 2000.

How can I mention Old Trafford without not mentioning Old Trafford Football stadium? The home of Manchester United FC is just a few minutes' walk from The Lowry.

When United were winning everything in sight I was foolish enough to bet with a lifelong Red I worked at the Messenger with, Dave, that City stood a chance of beating them in an up-and-coming derby match.

More often than not I tended to lose my money – because my team tended to lose the match.

But as City improved, so did my chance of getting a few quid back, which I did.

For the best part of two decades, I was among other things, Messenger's arts reporter. My pieces were shared with other titles in the group and for more than 20 years I had the luxury of writing about what I wanted.

In short, I'd landed my dream job.

Chapter 2

I started working at the paper on January 27, 1992. It was the day after my 27th birthday so, eager not to enter the world of work with a hangover, I was sensible when it came to my celebrations the night before.

The journey to Washway Road hadn't been an easy one. Did I think about giving up on my ambition? You bet I did.

As I was about to leave Sheffield University I experienced my first dose of disability discrimination, after applying for a place on a post-graduate training course in magazine journalism.

The course was based at a non-descript place down in Surrey called Sutton. After telling my interviewer I had good mobility, I received a bloody patronising letter saying to offer me a place would be cruel and unkind because the course required students to be able to get around quickly so they could get to classes.

The guy who interviewed me had obviously been thumbing through the Great Big Book of Excuses before he wrote his sod off letter.

What really rubbed salt into my wounds was the letter also said I was more than academically qualified to be offered a place on the course.

It was my experience with the magazine course and me narrowly escaping a boring job in the civil service that made me chase my journalistic dream.

There are some career paths people with disabilities are expected to follow and this really pisses me off.

Surely, the main point in going to university is the fact it gives you a choice over which career path you can take. Doesn't it?

But I was determined not to let the setback I suffered when I was applying for a place on the magazine course and my close encounter with boredom put me off.

So, I spent two and a half years freelancing for various publications, including the Messenger, hoping to get my foot in the door that way. I had developed a keen interest in live theatre, so it seemed logical to write about this newly acquired interest as a reviewer and a writer of previews. That was September 1987, and I haven't paid for a theatre ticket since. I still review productions on my blog, stagestruck.info, on both the amateur and professional stage in Trafford and Manchester respectively.

My freelance career included a trip to the Edinburgh Festival in 1988 which I used to also review a couple of plays being performed by a group of actors from Altrincham Garrick.

My best friend San and I saw more than 30 plays in eight days, and everything was going very smoothly until our landlady flipped one night after the couple's Alsatian dog ripped up her much-cherished kitchen.

She spent most of the night wailing like a banshee and San and I, her nerves shot to pieces, did the world's quickest flit back to Manchester after breakfast the following day. We left after leaving the couple a cheque to cover our outstanding board and lodgings behind the clock on their mantelpiece.

It was really sad because we'd got to really know the city and felt very comfortable there. But every cloud has a silver lining, and I used this unsettling experience as a basis for my play, A Long Day's Journey Into A Nightmare.

Further freelance work followed with Greater Manchester Theatre Magazine, Uptown and the newsletter of the disability arts organisation, North West Shape. Then there was Manchester's legendary listings magazine City Life, which saw me again write theatre reviews and features on subjects as varied as museum exhibitions and disability sport.

Founded initially as a co-operative, it was a very forward-thinking magazine that covered subjects the rest of the media didn't touch back then, like disability sport.

I also wrote for Uptown magazine which had a similar remit to City Life. But it was really it's poor relation, it wasn't as well produced and didn't have its reputation.

City Life was later taken over by the Manchester Evening News. I would have killed for a job there. But there were only three full-time journalists and I had to content myself with being one of a number of freelance contributors.

But even managing to become a regular freelance contributor was a real feather in my cap because City Life was so well thought of and a formidable champion of all things Greater Manchester.

Its famous graduates include the writer and broadcaster Jon Ronson who co-wrote the film Frank, loosely based on Frank Sidebottom, who I mentioned earlier.

The respected film critic Mark Kermode was also a regular contributor.

None of these publications exist now – with the exception of the Messenger – but they all played an important part in allowing me to build up an impressive cuttings book. But I was still no closer to getting that elusive reporting job.

I also worked for the newsletter run by the Greater Manchester and Lancashire Council on Alcohol.

The GMLCA had office space in a Victorian building in Manchester city centre that was directly opposite The Victoria pub. Ironically. The job was created as part of the Government's community programme and it was while working at the charity that I met George, a graphic designer, who had been recruited to work on the layout of the newsletter we'd been taken on to create.

George – I never knew his surname – was a gay man who had a wicked sense of humour. We'd only known each other for a matter of months. However, I felt devastated when he died. George had had quite a career before he came to the GMLCA because he designed numerous record sleeves for classical artists.

The organisation, now known by a different name, was run by a lovely lady called Liz Smith whose husband Ian worked for The Times. He had MS and was very encouraging when Liz told him I was trying to get into journalism. I remember Ian telling me he felt he could talk to me as an equal after he'd become disabled himself.

Ian also told me it didn't matter if you crawled to interviews as long as you wrote stories and articles that were good enough to sell papers or magazines. Unfortunately, I found that not to be the case and still feel that in spite of the anti-discrimination legislation disabled people are still at the bottom of the heap when it comes to jobs and the companies set up to help us are still fucking useless.

I even took to pounding the streets in a bid to get that elusive job in journalism and remember dropping into the Altrincham and Sale Guardian to see its Editor. The meeting was unplanned. The Guardian, which no longer exists, was part of the same group as the Messenger and I thought the paper's boss would have a vague inkling of who I was.

I showed him a copy of a news story which I'd written, and he said he liked it. Unfortunately, that was the only conversation we had.

As I tried to get that elusive job as a reporter, I experienced discrimination from an unlikely source. I'd been to London where I met the Editor of Disability Now, the magazine for The Spastics Society. We'd had what I thought was a really constructive meeting and after thumbing through my cuttings book, she said "You're good, aren't you?"

While I've never been one to blow my own trumpet, I replied to what was on reflection a rhetorical question with a tentative "yes" in a bid to project an air of confidence and self-belief.

I'd made the trip south to see if the charity had any openings for budding journalists like me. The meeting was going well, and things improved even more when the Editor offered me an assignment to cover a visit by the late Princess Diana to a charity event in Liverpool.

In case any note taking was needed I took San, a lifelong friend of mine, as my scribe. The Editor said that meant I wasn't cut out to be a journalist because if I went on a similar job, I would need to take another journalist. Maybe she was right.

Maybe I should just carry on with journalism as a hobby, carry on reviewing plays and shows at the theatres, keep taking the free tickets and the complimentary glass of booze at the interval.

It was a nice little number, after all.

But one thing my time at the Messenger taught me is there was a whole host of jobs I could do which *didn't* require shorthand. I can't remember the last time I watched the news on TV and saw a journalist scribbling away furiously on a notepad. Most of them use a tape recorder or a Dictaphone in order to get 'the story.'

Evidently the then Editor of DN didn't buy into my parents' philosophy about there being no such things as problems there are only solutions, and it was her negative outlook I found most frustrating.

With hindsight and bearing in mind my additional care needs, I'm not sure a move to London would have been realistic anyway. I also regard myself as a genetic northerner and would probably have felt like a fish out of water had I moved to the big city. But there's no getting away from the fact that most jobs in journalism are in the South East.

I had another fruitless trip to the capital when a magazine called City Limits had asked me to interview the eminent neurologist, Dr Oliver Sacks. Sacks was played in the film Awakenings, which remains one of the most moving pieces of cinema I've ever seen. We got on really well – it was impossible not to warm to this gentle, kind, un-assuming man.

He'd just written a new book and the interview took place at a posh hotel in the centre of London, complete with a concierge who actually opened the door of my cab when I arrived and when I was leaving.

I remember asking the delightful Dr Sacks if he'd ever been disturbed by some of the more severe neurological conditions he'd come into contact with, and his measured response made a lasting impression on me because he said what he found much more disturbing was the way in which human beings treat one another.

After my 400-mile round trip City Limits didn't use my interview on the grounds it was 'too pedestrian.' What the hell?

I would strongly advise against anybody going down the freelance route, including people with disabilities.

Speaking from experience, the competition is fierce and if a newspaper or magazine accepts your work, they don't rush to pay you, either.

You also have to be prepared to work a 7-day week and I wasn't prepared to do that and more importantly I wasn't physically capable of it.

So, what gave me the motivation to carry on and become a journalist? Well, living at home and not having bills to pay definitely helped.

Maybe the ridicule I endured while growing up and in adult life played a part in me eventually achieving my career goal.

It certainly didn't feel like it at the time, especially when I was a teenager trying to convey a cool image. But maybe it ended up being a positive influence in my life. Add to that my cast iron sense of determination and the unwavering support of my parents, family and friends who were far more influential when it came to helping me get what I wanted out of life.

I left secondary school without a full appreciation of just how important qualifications were and I could also be lazy at times. But when I went to sixth form college the penny dropped and I worked. My A levels, Sociology, Psychology and English Literature, remain the hardest exams I've ever sat.

Chapter 3

My luck finally turned in 1990. I had been on the books of the Shaw Trust, an employment agency for people with disabilities, when my employment officer at the job centre heard the Royal Association for Disability and Rehabilitation – RADAR – was offering bursaries to train budding disabled journalists.

The Shaw Trust looked into the scheme for me and told me how to apply. I applied for a place on the course at Sheffield.

Armed with my cuttings book I headed back over the Snake Pass to my spiritual home for an interview and I later received a letter a few weeks later offering me a place. I always think of Sheffield as my second home, the people are warm and friendly, except in winter when they're cold and friendly.

These days winter in South Yorkshire is generally a mild and tame affair due to the advent of global warming. A far cry from my university days when the snow was so deep that the buses would stop and there would be an inch or two of ice on the inside of my bedroom window at my student house.

But I digress.

Stradbroke College, where the course was held back then, was called a 'college' while in reality it felt more like a glorified secondary school. But that was irrelevant. I was there purely to pass my exams and get *that* job.

My journalism training was really helpful in that it helped me fine tune my news sense and improve the quality of my writing in general.

It also gave me an insight into the workings of local and national government. We also had to learn about the Law.

Law was definitely the most difficult of all the subjects we studied, and I felt even more depressed when Rod, our tutor, once told us what we were learning was only the equivalent of a GCSE in the subject. This left me very much in awe of those clever souls who take Law at degree level and end up making a career out of it.

By far the most boring part of my training involved learning about the workings of local and national government in a subject called Public Admin. It was dry. It was dull. But it was something we had to learn about. But you can't polish a turd, as the old saying goes and I felt very joyous when I had to use the Public Admin textbook for reference only when I was at work.

Journalism often requires you to work to tight deadlines and one of the most challenging assignments we had was to write a new story from a sheet of information in just 40 minutes. All the information was jumbled up in terms of priority and we had minutes to decide which points were the most important. It was a tough task. But it was a challenge I rose to.

We were also taught how not to over write by using the 'Fresh Fish Sold Here' test. Basically, we were asked to imagine these words were on a sign outside a fish shop and we had to decide which words were not needed in the sign. Have a go – if the inclination takes you.

I started at Stradbroke in January 1991. The course has two intakes, with students either doing an academic year, from September to July, or a calendar year, from January to December. My housemates, Andy and Dave, lived with me until the summer term. We hit it off instantly and I couldn't have picked better if I'd chosen them myself.

We had the same sense of humour and it was like the three of us had been mates forever. It was almost like we'd been separated at birth.

Unfortunately, I was on the calendar year course which meant Andy and Dave, who started the September before me, had left when I still had a term to go. The lads I lived with for my final term were ok. But they weren't really my kind of people, so I cut the amount of time I spent at Richmond Road to a minimum.

Andy, a broadly spoken Yorkshire lad who loved heavy rock and woke the house up with a blast of his favourite music every morning. But we didn't care.

He was also a big, big fan of Sheffield Wednesday and before going to a game one night actually hid his stereo under the table in the living room. The table was covered by a black cloth, so Dave and I didn't see it as we settled down to watch TV that night.

Andy's stereo had a timer fitted to it and, all of a sudden, we heard these Sheffield Wednesday songs blurting out and couldn't work out where they were coming from until Dave put two and two together and lifted up the cloth!

Hilarious.

What also helped me settle in was the fact the end cottage was occupied by Eamon and Sue who I'd gone to sixth form with.

The course lasted three full days and one morning a week we had Monday off. This was to give people who wanted to a chance to work said Ron, the course's larger than life director.

It was while I was at Stradbroke that I became *the* story.

Back in the 90s, Channel 4 screened a disability programme called Same Difference and its makers wanted to do a piece on the new RADAR journalism bursaries. I've always hated being in the limelight and I cringed when the cameras started rolling.

The first part of the programme saw me interview Helen Sharman's dad on camera. She was the first woman from the UK to go into space and I began the interview by asking him how he felt when he watched his daughter's rocket blast off. The sight of a TV camera made me feel very nervous.

The second part involved a trip to Sheffield's famous Crucible Theatre, and I felt far more relaxed as a result of the couple of pints of lager I'd supped in the theatre bar with my lunch. An equally important part of a journalist's training, some might say.

I still see Mark Todd, the reporter who interviewed me for Same Difference, on my way back from Man City home games.

As journalism students we also had to cover the meetings at Eckington Parish Council – which was an experience. The sleepy Derbyshire village is just outside Sheffield and the meetings reminded me so much of The Vicar of Dibley, the BBC sitcom starring Dawn French. The councillors were very broad, and this made what they said sound even funnier.

I can remember us trying to stifle the sniggers when an elderly councillor suddenly piped up: "I would like to raise the subject of skid marks – outside the village hall."

Comedy gold.

However, I was very grateful to the clerk of the council who agreed to meet me when they weren't having meetings and keep me up to speed with various news items. I taped our meetings, and I was grateful for his support.

One event he told me about was a concert by The Drifters which sent the women in the audience wild, apparently.

I would do my college work on an electric typewriter and an AMSTRAD computer was kept for any work I had to do back at the cottage.

At Stradbroke we also were asked to cover a cycle race through Sheffield and I can remember Kev, one of my student pals, asking a guy watching the event, clad head to foot in cycling gear and actually sitting astride a bike, whether he was into cycling. "No – I bloody hate it," he said, with trademark Yorkshire wit.

My other main college chum was Pete Devine, who achieved national acclaim for his coverage of the Harold Shipman case.

One of my main inspirations while at college was a lecturer called Tony Fry. Like me, he faced a challenge when it came to verbal communication because he spoke using a voice box. Tony was very encouraging, telling me to keep going and chase the dream.

Working as a reporter is definitely more interesting than training to do it. But the course helped me to write better copy – journalism speak for stories and articles.

I even ended up writing a piece for Disability Now about the RADAR bursary scheme and the way it helped me get into journalism, in a bid to inspire other people with disabilities to get into the industry.

Looking back at my 12 months in Sheffield, I recalled how I wasn't treated with 'kid gloves' by the tutors who expected me to meet the same project deadlines as my fellow trainees had to meet.

I was offered a place on the NCTJ course on one condition – that I would be offered a job at the end of it. The NCTJ want to know there was an employer out there who felt I would be able to hack it – no pun intended – in a busy newsroom.

The college was pretty forward thinking when it came to things like disabled access and while it's an issue that's never really affected me directly, I was impressed by the number of wheelchair friendly loos and ramps I saw around the place.

Its famous graduates include the former Top Gear presenter Jeremy Clarkson, and it was known as Richmond College back then.

While I was the most 'obviously' disabled student, there had been people with epilepsy and heart conditions who had gone before me.

The Messenger had promised me *that* job if I passed the course and I did.

Chapter 4

I can remember my first day at the paper like it was yesterday. In reality, it was nearly 30 years ago.

The first person I met was Carol, one of the copy typists, and she was lovely. After a brief tour of the kitchen, it was upstairs to meet my other colleagues. There was Phil, the Editor. He was funny, fun, and very northern, even down to his penchant for fish and chips.

I knew Phil from my freelance days and my repeated trips to the office. So, my familiarity with the place and most of the people who worked there meant I almost instantly felt at home.

Then there was the unforgettable Ollie Batchelor, a part-time reporter who had worked for the Daily Mirror, no less. Ollie invited us for lunch at his place one day and we enjoyed a feast fit for a king.

Mike, one of the sub-editors, was also our motoring correspondent and the principal perk of the job was he got to road test some rather swish top of the range cars. If being given a lift home in a Porsche wasn't enough, I've never forgotten the night he took me back to Altrincham in a Rolls Royce. If I had to compare the experience it was like travelling in a luxurious armchair. It really was *that* comfortable and I felt like a celebrity as Mike drove me home to Altrincham that night, attracting more than a few admiring glances from passers-by.

'Grum' as we called him, was also a very funny man with a very dry sense of humour. He was a serial pipe smoker, wore a sports jacket with leather elbow patches and tended to say "Right Oh" at the end of most of his sentences.

When I first joined the Messenger, I was the only male on the news desk, sitting next to Mel, Kay, Liz and another sub-editor, Lynn. Then there was Simon, the sports reporter and three photographers.

This included the rather gruff and bad-tempered senior photographer called John who I upset one hot summer day by taking his fan, oblivious to the fact it was his, to my desk in the main office in a bid to cool down. "I didn't know it was yours," I said, pleading innocence. "Didn't you see it had my name on it?" he growled, pointing to a sticker.

'Fan gate' proved to be short lived and John made a real effort to be extra nice to me after that. I can only assume Phil overheard John – who we all nicknamed Mr Magoo – explode in front of me and had a quiet word with him after our confrontation.

I could say the whole thing blew over. Get it?

Then there was Andrew – not his real name – a born again Christian who we took pleasure in winding up particularly about the pleasures of the flesh. It was a subject he was particularly uptight about. But I have to say I really admired Andrew for the way he stuck to his beliefs even in the face of frequent good humoured flak.

That takes guts.

But it didn't stop one of my colleagues planting a soft porn mag in his desk drawer while he was out of the office on an appointment one day. Andrew threw it across the office when he found it. But he did so with a half-smile, which made me think he saw the funny side of the schoolboy prank.

I was, with hindsight, getting into newspaper journalism at both the right and wrong time. The fax machine was particularly useful back in the early days because it allowed me to warn the people I was going to be interviewing about my speech. It could also be used to arrange celebrity interviews by enabling me to tell press officers and other publicity people about my problem when it came to verbal communication.

Email was also a Godsend because it meant I could do the same thing. But if I was facing a particularly pressing deadline, I would phone people up and nine times out of ten there weren't any problems when it came to making myself understood.

Then there was the good old-fashioned letter – does anyone remember them? I would write to potential interviewees and ask them to ring me up so we could make arrangements. Once we'd made contact, I'd always ask them if they wanted me to call them straight back, so the call wouldn't cost them anything more than a nominal amount of money.

Who knows, mentioning my speech impediment may have worked to my advantage because it aroused an additional sense of curiosity among potential interviewees. Maybe.

I remember meeting someone in the press bar at a theatre in Manchester one night when I was freelancing and told him I was an aspiring journalist. He was really encouraging and said my disability might end up being an advantage because maybe people I was interviewing would regard me as being less of 'a threat.'

Maybe he was right.

Ultimately, the introduction of the World Wide Web ended up being a mixed blessing because the Internet would ultimately start to eat into our advertising revenue which is the lifeblood of papers like the Messenger.

While I always found face to face interview easier, if I had to interview over the phone, I would simply put the phone on loudspeaker and record the conversation using my trusty pocket tape recorder.

The afore mentioned device became my 'shorthand' and one advantage it gave me was I could never be accused of misquoting an interviewee.

Doing interviews in a busy and noisy office could be difficult at times because I used a speaker phone. So, I came up with the bright idea of borrowing the advertising manager's office because Roger spent a large chunk of his working week out on the road.

I would go downstairs, plug my phone in and replace it with his once I'd finished.

A few weeks after joining the Messenger I was moved to a quieter corner of the office which made interviewing people over the phone easier. I shared my new home with Pete, the sports reporter, and Jude, his copy typist.

It later become known as the naughty boy's corner – for reasons that were never really explained to me.

Pete and I became really good mates, and this included a memorable trip to London to watch Altrincham get battered by Spurs 4-1 in the FA Cup. Great banter, good beer. The only thing that would have made the day 100 per cent perfect would have been a giant killing.

Back then I'd still not forgiven Spurs for beating City in the 1981 FA Cup Final at the time. But time is a great healer, as they say, and I can now hold my hands up and say Ricky Villa's winning goal was pure class.

When I interviewed celebrities, I never went into interview with a long list of questions because I found this far too constricting and there was also a chance an interview could throw up something unexpected.

This is less true of news stories which are more issue or issues based.

While writing news stories formed the bulk of my training, I always felt more comfortable with features and reviews. When writing features, you can generally be more creative which meant Messenger's glossy Lifestyle magazine was an ideal outlet for my talents. Even if I knew nothing at all about interior design!

A career in magazine journalism would, with hindsight, probably have suited me better. But the course I applied for in Surrey only had publications in Birmingham and London. Bearing in mind my additional care needs, that would have been a non-starter for little old me.

Initially, the Messenger promised me a job on its Stockport edition if I passed the NCTJ course. But the powers that be felt it would be easier for me to go to the paper that covered the area I knew and knew well.

While I was fortunate enough to interview scores of famous people, my first job as a member of staff was far from glamorous. It involved a trip to interview staff at Tyrell's fishmongers in Altrincham.

One of the workers, oblivious to the double entendre, told me he used to work in Cornwall where he caught crabs, a comment which caused much hilarity back at the office.

Very childish I know, but what the hell.

"Don't worry Rick – I'm sending you to the sewage farm next week," joked Phil, my Editor.

As a reporter it's important to be versatile and never turn your nose up at stories that aren't initially so appealing.

One such assignment came when I was asked to interview a lady from Sale who collected rocks as a hobby. There were one or two interesting and colourful items in her collection. But it was a real test of my journalistic skills to turn what is, let's face it, a niche hobby into a subject that would have interested our thousands of readers. But I did it.

Nor can I forget the president of one of the local rotary clubs who, despite the good work carried out by the organisation, evidently wasn't in the room when they were handing out personalities.

There are stories like planned changes to bin collections by the council, stories that are very important to the readership.

No two days are ever the same when you work on newspapers which was one aspect of the job I found particularly enjoyable.

For example, I could be writing about bin collections one day and a preview of The Ladyboys of Bangkok the next.

I remember seeing this amazing troupe of performers when they brought their glitzy revue show to The Lowry in Salford and thinking how stunning they looked, before I realised, they were actually *men*.

More importantly, the show, a sparkly sea of sequins, elaborate costumes, and fans, is a really good night out.

Ironically, it was stories and features with a nostalgia theme that aroused the most interest from Messenger readers when I was there. A classic case in point were the several pieces I wrote about Chapel Street in Altrincham, which I'll come to later.

All I needed to interview people was a phone fitted with a loudspeaker and my trusty tape recorder.

This meant I did exactly the same job as my colleagues. I just did it differently, that's all.

My career at the paper didn't get off to a very good start and left me wondering if my doubters had been right all along. When I was trying to get into journalism an excuse frequently trotted out by various people was that my verbal communication just wasn't good enough.

The first interview I organised off my own bat was a piece on alternative medicine which was becoming increasingly fashionable in the 1990s.

I rang up the practice that was virtually on our doorstep and had the receptionist put the phone down on me. Apparently, she'd just had a funny phone call and assumed the culprit who was a woman, had decided to put a man of the line. This was one of the first interviews I'd arranged off my own bat and I found the experience deeply disconcerting.

Ollie was in the office, and he picked up on my awkwardness and agreed to ring the practice on my behalf in order to explain my situation.

I had visions of being shown the door early which was somewhat disrespectful to my bosses who remained very supportive on the rare occasions I encountered the ignorant.

But an interview was arranged, the doctor got a plug for his practice, and I got a free session of reflexology and an apology from the doc who explained the reason behind the receptionist's behaviour.

There were one or two 'bumps' in the road. One caller actually asked my Editor if I was drunk after I'd put his call through to him.

The nature of our phone system also meant there were occasions when reporters took advertising calls and vice versa.

I can remember one such call, and an advertising customer asked me if I was 'taking the piss' when I was speaking to him because he evidently thought I was putting on some kind of comedy voice. He even threw in an 'f-bomb' before the 'piss' part.

We met a few days later and it was evident that one of our advertising team had put him in the picture about my disability. Cue the grovelling. This guy apologised to me profusely, shaking my hand so frenziedly I felt as if it was going to fall off!

These blips never stopped me interviewing hundreds and hundreds of people as a reporter. While I always found face to face interviews a lot easier than those I did on the phone, nine times out of ten I completed the task in hand.

But it isn't easy for someone with a speech impediment to speak to strangers over the phone, let alone interview them.

While I was at the Messenger, I was lucky enough to interview some fabulous, fascinating and inspirational people, from playwright Alan Bennett to former Church of England envoy Terry Waite to the writer and comedian Ben Elton and former Culture Club lead singer Boy George.

So, the number of people who couldn't understand me was far outweighed by the number who could.

I also managed to secure some phone time with a rock legend in the shape of ex-Rolling Stones bassist Bill Wyman about an up-and-coming gig with his band, The Rhythm Kings in 2013 at the Bridgewater Hall in Manchester. Unfortunately, there was one subject that was off limits for the veteran star. The Rolling Stones. Life's just not fair, is it?

I was desperate to hear from the veteran musician what it's really like to live *the* rock 'n' roll lifestyle for decades and how he'd managed to survive it. But I had to content myself with the revelations that he hated the idea of hanging up that famous bass of his and retiring and the fact he would have been a professional cricketer had he not chosen a career in pop.

There were other interviewees who set their own agenda and I was told by their press people not to touch certain subjects. It still baffles me to this day why the actor Don Warrington refused point blank to talk about the role of Philip in the seminal sitcom Rising Damp. After all it was the part that helped launch his tv career. Yet he was more than happy to appear on a recent Channel 4 documentary extolling the programme's virtues.

Shown in the 1970s when attitudes to everything were considerably less enlightened than they are today, most of Rising Damp took place in a series of crumby bedsits overseen by that dictator in a cardigan, the landlord Rigsby.

As well as having short arms and very deep pockets, Rigsby was also an incurable racist. But it was Warrington's character, the smooth and suave Philip, who ran rings around the old miser. When the programme was shown, BAME actors like Don Warrington were rarely seen on our TV screens.

Surely that deserves to be celebrated?

Thankfully, such interviews were at a premium.

I had two memorable encounters with Danny Boyle, the award winning, Manchester born film director. The enthusiasm the bubbly Boyle has for his work is infectious, without spilling over into irritating affectation. I met him twice at the now gone Cornerhouse art and cinema complex in Manchester. He came across as really genuine and as the sort of bloke who'd be just as much at home standing at the bar of his local pub as he'd be at a star-studded film premiere.

I also liked the way he showed a genuine interest in what our work experience student was studying when I met him for the first time. Scores of celebrities have a favourite subject – themselves – and would happily witter on about 'themselves' for hours.

We met for the first time when the multi-award-winning filmmaker – at the time of meeting he'd picked up more than 22 awards – returned to his home city to promote Shallow Grave. I still can't understand to this day why this claustrophobic thriller received such a lukewarm response in critical circles.

The second meeting was part of a round of interviews he was doing for Sunshine in 2005 and he was on the verge of starting work on Slumdog Millionaire. For those who haven't seen it, it's the fascinating true story of a young lad who takes part in the Hindi version of Who Wants To Be A Millionaire – and wins. The fact this boy is from the wrong side of the social tracks attracts the suspicion of the authorities and the police, who believe he's a cheat and start torturing him.

While Boyle's own work has won him a host of awards and many, many admirers, he's a fan of the director Nick Roeg whose credits included The Man Who Fell To Earth, the cult classic starring pop icon David Bowie.

Chapter 5

The advice I would give to any budding journalists is simple - try to put yourself in the shoes of the reader when carrying out interviews and ask the questions you feel the readers want to ask. But there's one thing I remember from my days at Stradbroke – don't be scared to divert from the subject you initially set out to cover in the first place. This unwritten commandment can also be applied to news and sports stories as well as feature articles.

It's also important to put people at their ease. I can remember seeing a master at work, when I was at the alcohol charity and I went to Granada TV to watch my boss, Liz being interviewed by John Huntley, one of the presenters at the Manchester based TV channel. Going in front of a camera isn't something you do every day – unless you had a job like his of course.

In a bid to quell her natural nerves, he turned to her and said, quietly, "Just pretend you're talking to me." I tried a similar tactic whenever I met someone who froze at the sight of my tape recorder and were anxious not to say the wrong thing.

There are invariably jobs you're asked to do that require an extra dose of sensitivity. One such assignment fell into my lap when I had to interview a couple from Sale whose only son had died in a motorcycle accident. Being an emotional person at the best of times I was dreading the visit to their flat and I told the photographer how I was feeling.

His response was, "Just imagine how they feel," he said. This remark really brought me to my senses and made me stop being so fucking selfish. The couple talked about their son which was deeply humbling as he sounded like a really good guy and the type of person this world needs.

I would even go as far as to say they found it a cathartic experience.

But most of my career I spent doing features and celebrity interviews and it was probably the field in which I felt the most comfortable. It was certainly the area in which I was at my journalistic best.

Okay, I'll admit it. I was a self-conscious kid, mainly because of my disability.

I was uncomfortable even by the prospect of meeting celebrities and now I was earning a living interviewing them. It wasn't a major problem for me, growing up in Sale rather than LA. I remember when I met Steve Daley, the ex-Man City player, after the Bowen clan had finished a pub meal. I cringed with embarrassment as I approached the table he was sitting at to ask him for his autograph.

Daley's big money move from Wolves was an unmitigated disaster and his stay at the club was a brief one. Daley had been signed by Malcolm Allison; the charismatic former club coach who had been brought in as manager in the late 70s in a bid to revive the fortunes of a struggling team.

Allison, charismatic and cigar toting, had been one half of the legendary Mercer/Allison partnership which saw City win five trophies in the late 60s and early 70s. But that's the point. He was part of a hugely successful *partnership* and it's always a mistake to 'go back' isn't it?

When it comes to football, I am the black sheep of a family almost entirely made up of Man United fans. Why did a choose City then? The main reason was you never knew what you were going to get from the Blues. I'm talking before our glory days. I can actually remember seeing them on TV a few days after my son James was born and they lost 3-2 at home to the mighty Stockport County!

Maybe I've also been drawn to the plight of the underdog. But those days have been long consigned to the history books after City received a huge injection of Abu Dhabi cash. Doesn't that make you feel uncomfortable, many a fan of Man United has asked me since the takeover of the club by Sheikh Mansour? Er, no.

My own footballing prowess is, you'll be surprised to discover, rather limited. I can play football - as long as nobody tries to tackle me. I can't run, either. But I do have a powerful left foot. I can remember two girls sniggering at me playing five a side at secondary school only for yours truly to score twice and silence the sniggers. *But they still substituted me!* Where is a bottle of pop – I don't think they had bottled water back then – to kick to show your frustration?

But I never really cared that I wasn't any good at sport.

It may surprise you to know – it bloody well surprised me – that I am really good at crazy golf. That may sound bloody ridiculous coming from somebody who wasn't even in the queue when the Good Lord handed out co-ordination. I put all this down to the time I'd spent as a kid on the putting green at Ashton Park. In my head I was playing in the Open. In reality, I was simply playing in the open air.

While blue blood coasts swiftly through my footballing veins I can remember being asked to write a piece for the Messenger website on the eve of the Manchester derby at Old Trafford in 2008, which also just happened to be the 50th anniversary of the Munich air crash. The piece reminded City fans to respect one of sport's most sombre of occasions while living up to our 'noisy neighbours' tag and roaring the Blues on to victory.

There are some things that are far more important than football.

I actually went to Old Trafford when City beat United 2-1 thanks to Pete, a friend of my auntie who managed to get me a ticket – in the United end. The funniest thing was when the final whistle blew, one of the blokes I was with put a consoling arm around me and said "Don't worry Rick, we'll win next time." Obviously, I'd kept my true colours a secret or I would have been ejected from the ground. But I couldn't resist a wry smile as I made my way back to enjoy a few post-match pints courtesy of Pete.

What struck me during my afternoon with the Reds was how many supporters around me sat there and slated Sir Alex Ferguson for some of his decision making throughout the game. I was shocked and appalled by that. After all, you're only talking about the most successful managers football has ever seen. What does he know?

I was also struck by the lack of leg room I had at what is supposed to be one of the country's most iconic grounds. Even a shorty like me, at a towering five foot five inches, struggled to get comfortable.

My favourite interview while I was at the Messenger has to be the half an hour I had with Terry Waite, the former Church of England envoy who was kidnapped by terrorists in the Lebanon and held in solitary confinement for 1763 days – nearly 5 years.

Articles like these just write themselves and the phone time I had with Waite flew by. I joked how I could have talked to him all day as the interview was drawing to a close and that made him laugh heartily.

His life affirming story of survival was set to music and he shared his experiences at the Avenue Methodist Church in Sale in 2003 as part of a fundraiser for the charity Cancer Research UK.

An even greater thrill came when my contact at the church gave me a complimentary ticket for the event and offered me a chance to meet this remarkable figure.

Meeting this gentle big bear of a man was an experience I'll never forget, and I snapped up the offer with all the unbridled enthusiasm of a child on Christmas morning.

Terry Waite was my most impressive interviewee for a variety of reasons, for the way in which he bore no malice towards his cruel captors who made him often endure the extra ordeal of mock executions.

Just imagine someone placing a hood over your head, cocking their gun, and then uncocking it seconds later, only to tell you they've suddenly changed their mind about killing you. How utterly terrifying must that feel?

When I met him, it was rather like coming face to face with a real life giant. But the fact he's six foot seven didn't stop his captors trying to move him to a new secret location dressed in a burka.

A burka is a piece of clothing usually worn by Muslim women that can cover the whole of the body. Despite his ordeal, this remarkable character could somehow see the funny side and raised a smile when he told me about the one lighter aspect of an otherwise nightmare ordeal.

Meeting this true survivor was very, very humbling, and certainly allowed me to get my own petty squabbles into perspective. When it comes to religion, I'm a member of the agnostic brigade these days. But Terry Waite is everything you would expect a true Christian to be. An example to us all.

Another memorable interview, for different reasons, was with the peace campaigner Colin Parry.

I met him when he visited Woodheys Primary School in Sale to open a peace garden in memory of a pupil there who had died from cancer.

Colin's son Tim, along with the toddler Jonathan Ball, were murdered by the IRA in Warrington. Inevitably the conversation turned as to whether Colin had forgiven former IRA commander turned politician Martin McGuiness for what happened to his son.

While Colin hadn't forgiven the IRA for the murder of Tim, he invited him to attend a forthcoming lecture organised by the charity he set up to work for reconciliation.

Meeting Colin Parry was a memorable experience.

The word *genius* is scandalously overused these days. However, I can't think of a better way to describe Alan Bennett. My admiration for him and his work goes back to the 1980s when I saw him on stage in London in one of his plays.

More than a decade later I was fortunate enough to be in the audience when he came to South Trafford College in Timperley to read extracts from his work. It was a special evening in the company of a very special man who refuses still to take the adulation he receives with anything other than an endearing sense of modesty.

This celebrated national treasure uses dialogue to paint vivid pictures inside your head and I challenge anyone not to be moved by Bennett's account of a trip he made to see his mam after she'd been admitted to a psychiatric hospital.

This harrowing account, which can be found in his collection Untold Stories, broke my heart completely.

It seemed from reading it, that all the patients had been lumped together on the same ward, regardless of the severity of their conditions.

On a lighter note, when he visited South Trafford, he read a piece about a group of women and a visit to a posh department store in Leeds and the way it brought out the snob in all of them. I could picture them swanning about the place, with their noses in the air.

He also has a gift when it comes to writing about the minutiae of life in a way that leaves the listener captivated.

I hoped he would agree to an unscheduled interview. However, his schedule was tight on that particular evening, and we had to content ourselves with a photo.

But the best things come to those who wait, as the old saying goes.

When we spoke, Alan Bennett was promoting his new play, People, which came to The Lowry in Salford in September 2015. The piece was used in the Guardian – the Knutsford one rather than the national one – which is one of our sister papers.

At the end of the interview, he said to me, with all the breathy enthusiasm of a writer starting out, "I hope you like my new play." This comment floored me completely, but I managed to think on my feet and reply, "Well, your others haven't been so bad, Alan." He laughed, heartily.

I just felt I'd been given a lesson in how to be humble by a man who is this country's greatest living playwright. If he does have an ego, he keeps it well and truly hidden.

Alan also told me he finds it easier to write dialogue for women rather than men as he grew up in the north of England, in an all-female household where it was the women who did all the talking. Professionally he also revealed he had a soft spot for Thora Hird, who starred in one of his critically acclaimed monologues, A Cream Cracker Under The Settee.

Another 'scoop' came when, after numerous calls to his agent, the comedian, actor, and writer Steve Coogan turned up to our office for an interview. I remember the Manchester born star being quiet and unassuming and most unlike a 'star.' The promoter at Manchester's legendary comedy club The Buzz put me in touch with his agent and my steely determination did the rest.

It was the mid-90s and Coogan was driving a very nice car back then, so he must be minted by now.

I've never had a problem with celebrities blessed with a genuine talent making pots of money – good luck to them. But don't get me started on those who become famous after appearing on these moronic reality TV shows.

The interview with Coogan ended on a hilarious note with the remarkably versatile performer treating me to a number of impressions from his Spitting Image days.

His impression of Ronnie Corbett was particularly good and made me laugh far more than the real Ronnie Corbett ever did. Corbett's convoluted jokes, which he delivered on that leather office style chair during his TV shows with Ronnie Barker, seemed to go on longer than the Gettysburg Address and were never that funny anyway.

If it passed you by, Spitting Image was a satirical TV show which poked fun at everybody from politicians to the Royal Family and Steve Coogan was one of the impressionists who appeared on it. It was compulsive viewing for me and millions more.

It was Agraman, promoter of The Buzz, who put me in touch with Steve Coogan's agent.

Buzz comedy nights took place every Thursday at the Southern Hotel in Chorlton and were hosted by John Marshall who performed a puns-based comedy act under the stage name of Agraman. The agreeable host also came from Sale and I took no hesitation when it came to claiming him as one of our own.

It's hard to believe a venue that would host performances by the likes of comedy icons like Jo Brand and Peter Kay, actually started life in a tiny room above the Malt Shovels pub in Altrincham. For comedy fans like me The Buzz was as important as The Cavern Club is to pop fans from my parents' generation. The Southern also served the best pint of Boddington's bitter I've ever had. What was not to like?

Bill Bailey, recent winner of the BBC show Strictly Come Dancing, was also a regular there. The Buzz was simply one of the best nights out I've ever had and apart from an evening of top-class comedy I loved mixing with a student crowd again.

Not everyone who went to The Buzz was a student.

Agraman also put on a show at Wythenshawe Forum – a venue that's sadly now closed – featuring a then up and coming stand up called Frank Skinner. As a member of the tiny audience, I could see that here was a performer with plenty of promise. Skinner's career was very much in its infancy back then. But it was impossible not to be impressed by the standard of his delivery and his astute sense of comic timing.

Not all the funniest people I interviewed came from the world of stand-up comedy. James H Reeve hosted the legendary late-night phone-in show on

Piccadilly Radio in Manchester in the late 1980s. The way he destroyed the bigoted or spoke up for the marginalised was quite brilliant and I went to bed early with him whenever I was home from university.

A natural wit, James H was for me, the consummate broadcaster. I recently looked him up on YouTube when I was twiddling my thumbs before going to bed one night and I laughed until my sides hurt. I found it crass and insulting the way someone called him 'the real Alan Partridge' in the comments section at the bottom of the video. How very dare you!

Alan Partridge, for those who aren't familiar with him, is the comic creation of Steve Coogan, a broadcaster who suffered from foot in mouth disease and dreamt of a lucrative TV career. The reality is very different– he works the graveyard shift at Radio Norwich.

If ever you're searching for something to brighten your day, I recommend looking up James H Reeve on YouTube and listening to his Nocturnal Emissions. I guarantee you won't be disappointed.

I was always jealous of Jim for his confidence and the way he could cut idiots down to size with his verbal barbs. He was a master when it came to that and we also share similar politics, which was good.

One of the biggest pleasures I had in my career was the time I interviewed James H and Tommy Docherty when he and the ex-Man United manager presented the sports programme on Piccadilly Radio. There was a natural chemistry between the two which made the show a 'must not miss' on Saturday afternoons.

I was actually on my way to watch City at Maine Road afterwards and made the mistake of showing my season ticket to Jim in full view of the former Reds boss.

'The Doc' picked up on it and subjected me to a volley of good humour that included the old joke "Don't follow the crowd Rick – you'll end up in Tesco's."

Okay, it was an old gag. But it still made me laugh. Jim and The Doc were a wonderful double act and the only radio show to come close to theirs in terms of entertainment value has been The Sports Bar presented by Andy Goldstein and former Chelsea footballer Jason Cundy on weeknights. These two made the Coronavirus lockdown bearable for me by putting a smile on my little face every time I listen to them.

I was sad to hear about the recent death of Tommy Docherty who was without a shadow of a doubt one of football's great characters.

James H Reeve left his late-night phone-in show in 1989 and handed the baton to another James, James Stannage, who I also interviewed for the Messenger.

All broadcasters have their own inimitable style, of course. But this particular phone-in, broadcast on Piccadilly's sister station Key 103, had something of 'after the Lord's Mayor's show' about it.

When I interviewed the presenter, I struggled to warm to a man who didn't have the charisma of

James H Reeve and was about as subtle as a smack in the face when it came to being controversial on air.

I really enjoy the radio. I particularly like it for the way in which it fires my imagination. For many years I've listened to what has become a global broadcasting phenomenon I initially thought was too northern to have an appeal beyond these parts.

The Bradshaws. The famous radio family from Barnoldswick, Lancashire, were created by one Buzz Hawkins, then a producer at Piccadilly Radio, the Manchester based station on which their misadventures were first broadcast.

It was on the show hosted by Gary Davies, a DJ who was to go on to achieve national fame on Radio 1, that Alf, Audrey and Billy were heard for the first time in a poem about a day trip to Blackpool.

Alf, the dad, Audrey, the fusspot mum, and son Billy, inhabit a north of England that only exists in folk memory. A world in which the women dry stone their front steps and kids actually play out rather than sit glued zombie like to computer screens.

Before I met Buzz, I'd never realised it was he who voiced the characters. Previously, I'd thought the gruff sounding Alf was voiced initially by the late Liverpool actor Bill Dean, who played Harry Cross on the Scouse soap Brookside, for many years.

The show's appeal is worldwide and Buzz – whose real name happens to be Billy – said he receives orders for tapes extending from Barnoldswick to far flung locations like Bermuda.

They're also simple tales of family life and the invariable tussles between mam and dad and dad versus child. And these themes are both eternal and universal.

The kid in question is little Billy, who remains forever aged eight. The Bradshaws is totally inoffensive and fun listening for kids aged 8 to 88.

I don't like people who drone on about the 'good old days' because they were only 'good' if you had money and power.

For me, The Bradshaws reminds me of playing out with my mates on bogeys and going to the off-licence with empty pop bottles to claim 10p back on them.

A 'bogey' has nothing to do with the contents of the human nose. They were like a makeshift racing kart usually featuring pram wheels that you raced while trying to avoid injury. We called them bogeys when we were kids. But maybe 'glorified death traps' would have been a more suitable term.

One of my final interviews for the Messenger was with Mark Chapman, the Altrincham based presenter of Match of the Day 2. I grew up watching this TV programme with my dad, so I was really looking forward to interviewing the man who fronts the show on Sunday nights.

What immediately struck me when I met 'Chappers' over coffee in Altrincham market is how unaffected and ordinary he is for someone working in TV. But there's no doubting his immeasurable talent either and he seems able to strike a perfect balance between being informal and professional.

It's like you're watching three friends talking football in the pub. But the reality is very different and involves hours of rigorous planning.

Mark said a 12-hour working day is the norm when putting together the show. Which means any 'socialising' with the programme's pundits happens only on social media.

So, there's no chance of a pint afterwards.

A lifelong Man United supporter, high on 'Chappers' bucket list would have been the chance to play alongside Beckham, Giggs and Keane and Scholes in that all conquering Reds team of the 1990s.

The Rochdale born broadcaster is also a familiar face in the stands at Altrincham FC with his son, who really enjoys the up close and personal nature of the matches at Moss Lane.

Chapter 6

My biggest fear when interviewing the famous was a totally irrational one that they would fail to live up to expectations and be nothing like what I expected them to be.

Dave Ward, who comes from Urmston, was a familiar voice on Piccadilly Radio for many years across Greater Manchester and when I interviewed him, he recalled an interview he'd done with the legendary comedy actor Leonard Rossitter. Dave recalled how Rossitter said at the start of the interview: "I'm not a comedian, I'm a comedy actor."

I can also remember interviewing Neil Morrissey, who played the laddish layabout Tony in the 90's sitcom, Men Behaving Badly. Morrissey was appearing in Oliver at The Lowry and I somewhat foolishly expected him to be at least a bit like Tony and for us to have a laddish chat.

But the real Neil Morrissey is a study in maturity – nothing like his character in the afore mentioned sitcom.

The comedian behind Harry Hill isn't remotely wacky in real life and there was no sign of that zany TV persona that's a hallmark of his act.

In fact, when you speak to him, he seems sensible and unassuming.

I interviewed the comedian prior to the release of The Harry Hill movie in 2013. While its title wouldn't receive any prizes for originality the plot line certainly would. The plot sees Harry and his nan, played by the wonderful Julie Walters, embark on a road trip with a difference.

Harry thinks his hamster is on his last little legs and only has a week to live before heading for the great hamster wheel in the sky. So, he comes up with a bright idea of letting his furry friend achieve the things on his bucket list and drafts in his gran to help.

Walters is one of the best and most versatile actors this country has produced in my opinion. In fact, she's far more versatile than her late comedy partner Victoria Wood. While Wood was also very talented, she never really moved away from her homely brand of comedy, littered with 'in jokes' aimed at female members of her audience.

Harry Hill is the creation of Matthew Hall, a former doctor and father of three from Surrey. They say laughter is the best medicine, don't they? Just in case you're wondering what prompted this most dramatic of career changes, he said the long hours were a major factor and a working week of 100 hours became the norm for a man keen to try something else.

In terms of his own personal comedy 'bucket list' he'd love to work with Simon Bird of Inbetweeners fame and Ricky Gervais, who shot to fame after he played the incurably irritating David Brent in the classic cringe comedy The Office.

Personally, I thought The Office was the peak of his comedy career and that was until I watched Gervais in After Life on Netflix.

Funny and in places painfully moving, it's the story of a cynical and sarcastic newspaper reporter struggling to come to terms with the death of his partner from cancer.

So, Ricky is far more than just a one trick pony when it comes to comedy and anyone who needs further proof, watch Derek, in which he plays a man with learning difficulties who works at an old people's residential home.

There are, however, some celebrities who have a set spiel that they just won't stray from and others who insist on seeing your questions before the interview takes place and won't answer questions on anything else.

One of the most disappointing was with the former cricketer Phil Tuffnell who I interviewed to mark 25 years of the BBC sports quiz, A Question of Sport. It was as though Tuffers, as he's affectionately known in the show, was reading from a press release and I felt I could have got the same information from a press release, to be honest.

George Cole, a seasoned actor who was probably best known for playing slippery con man Arthur Daley in the ITV comedy drama Minder, was another interviewee who wouldn't go 'off script.'

Before the interview, organised to mark the release of a commemorative Minder DVD, his publicity person asked me to send the questions prior to our chat. I asked Mr Cole – he not once told me to ditch the formality – if he liked Daley. He said he did but wouldn't want to live next door to him!

While George Cole was as gentlemanly as you would expect him to be, there were three interviews that didn't come off due to the refusal of the interviewees to make allowances for my speech impairment. One was the comedy writer, Barry

Cryer, who was about to bring his one man show to Sale's Waterside Arts Centre.

I found him prickly, rude and unhelpful and as funny as a poke in the eye with a wet stick. He also refused point blank to give me his email address so he could send me written replies to my questions. The whole situation was bloody ridiculous – did he think I was going to send him photos of my privates or something?

Looking back, I think Cryer's blanket refusal to co-operate was partly due to the fact he didn't think ours was a publication that was worth bothering with.

After that unfortunate experience with him I always feel like throwing something at the TV whenever he appears on it and I'm sure his one-man show was a barrel of laughs – not!

The other interview from hell came courtesy of the singer Elkie Brooks who was just rude and ended up putting the phone down on me. In my naivety I thought we'd have a natural affinity because we both come from Greater Manchester but no, I wasn't worth making the effort for.

The third interview 'nasty' came courtesy of singer Russell Watson's publicity officer who mysteriously ditched me from the interview schedule after struggling to understand me when I called him to arrange my chat with RW.

I was told Watson didn't have time for my interview which was complete bullshit because a colleague told me a friend of his who worked on another paper managed to get an interview with him straight after the time slot that had been initially given to me.

While those experiences were deeply unpleasant, I didn't dwell on them and was able to dust myself off and go again. But I'd be lying if I said the experiences didn't knock my confidence for a short time at least.

My message to those who can't deal with disabled people is please bear in mind that being able bodied isn't necessarily permanent and can change in a matter of seconds.

For example, when I was at secondary school there was a girl – who I'm not going to name here – who ridiculed me at every given opportunity. She was involved in a car accident, suffered brain damage, and ended up with a condition very similar to mine.

All I've ever asked for from people is a little empathy and a willingness to actually listen to what I'm saying to them.

But change takes time.

For instance, when I was freelancing for City Life, they asked me to write an article about disability sport when disability sport didn't receive any coverage at all. Now, athletes with disabilities and their sporting achievements are regularly covered in the national press and on the TV news.

But the majority of celebrities and their publicity people I came into contact with were disarmingly pleasant and helpful.

These included the publicist who represented that quintessential English gent, Nigel Havers who gave me a face-to-face interview to promote a play he was in that was coming to The Lowry. Most of the other journalists had been told they had to put their questions to him in a press conference.

I always avoided press conferences for the simple reason there was always a chance I could be misunderstood. Another reason was at press conferences it's hard to steer an interview in the direction you want it to go in.

What a pity the production, Art was such a major disappointment despite the actor being part of a cast that included Denis Lawson and Stephen Tompkinson. The play, translated from French to English, was a boring and soulless affair with something of the emperor's new clothes about it.

I felt rather short-changed after sitting through Art. And I don't even pay for theatre tickets!

Art certainly wasn't the most tedious piece of theatrical torture I ever went through. That honour goes to a play called Rookery Nook by Ben Travers which should be compulsive viewing for anyone suffering from insomnia or for the parents of badly behaved kids desperately searching for a deterrent to ward off future tantrums.

This piece of dross has no plot and hardly anything happens which, feel free to correct me if I'm wrong, are pretty important things to have in a play. I reviewed Rookery Nook for the Messenger as a freelance and gave it an absolute slating, which prompted a pensioner to put pen to paper and write me a very angry letter.

Other productions from my own personal chamber of theatrical horrors include a play performed in Russian with English subtitles projected on to a screen above the stage, which made it impossible to focus on what was happening on it. The play in question also seemed to go on for about as long as the Russian Revolution itself.

One of the best professional productions I've ever seen include the wonderful, witty and at times deeply moving Torch Song Trilogy, starring a superb Lionel Haft. While the name might not men a great deal to you, you may remember him as the hen-pecked son of Maureen Lipman's Beatie character in the TV ads for British Telecom. Why Haft never became a massive star is beyond me and Harvey Fierstein's script remains one of the best modern scripts I've ever come across.

It took place at the much-loved Library Theatre.

The venue, once situated in the basement of Central Library in Manchester's St Peter's Square, staged its last production 10 years ago before it morphed into HOME, a venue it shared with Cornerhouse.

The staff at the Library Theatre were more like friends rather than press contacts when I went there to conduct an interview or review a production. I interviewed David Nielsen, known to millions of Coronation Street fans as the soap's wonderfully geeky but eminently lovable Roy Cropper. He was appearing in Samuel Beckett's obscure classic, Waiting for Godot.

It was funny – I could actually see traces of Roy Cropper in some of Neilson's mannerisms.

The LTC's famous alumni include Sir Anthony Hopkins and Harry Potter star Richard Griffiths, the latter gracing us with his presence at the company's farewell Gala Night. What a pity then, that Griffiths' heart didn't seem to be in it. It felt as though his short speech had been 'phoned in' to be honest.

The farewell show featured excerpts from musicals that had graced the stage there, including one of my personal favourites, Company. Its sister theatre, Wythenshawe Forum – now closed – was a centre of excellence when it came to producing top class musicals.

It was here that I met Chris Honer, for me the best director ever to work in my home city. Bad productions just aren't in this man's DNA and he made time for everybody, including me. On Gala Night there wasn't a programme waiting for me at the press desk so, Chris offered to get me one and he did. That may sound like a little thing. But the little things often go a long way, don't they?

Manchester is blessed with a variety of venues that cater for most theatrical tastes. There's the futuristic looking Royal Exchange that's witnessed stellar performances by acting heavyweights like Robert Lindsay and Vanessa Redgrave.

The Lowry, which I covered the official opening of, provides a programme that is an engaging mix of mainstream and cutting-edge live performances.

It was there that I interviewed the daughter of Hollywood icon Judy Garland, Lorna Luft, who told me the image of her late mom the public has is far removed from the person she knew. Ms Luft was in Salford to appear in the theatre's annual panto.

We also have the Palace Theatre and the Opera House which largely serves up a 'bums on seats' sort of programme.

With the exception of shows like Puppetry of the Penis, in which the cast used their privates to create some weird and wonderful shapes in a show that remains by far the weirdest I've ever sat through.

In short, we're spoilt rotten when it comes to live theatre and the arts in Greater Manchester.

In Trafford we're extremely lucky to have an equally strong, vibrant and increasingly adventurous amateur theatre scene. After spending more than 30 years reviewing the work of the so-called amateurs, I can safely say there's nothing amateurish about amateur theatre. In my experience there's little to choose between what they produce and what's produced on the professional stage.

Altrincham Garrick is two venues in one, with the main stage devoted to productions with a largely mass appeal and the Lauriston Studio, its sister venue, putting on more cutting-edge stuff for anyone looking for an intimate theatrical experience.

The same is also true of Altrincham Little Theatre which has just over 120 seats and an uncanny ability to put on plays that fall into the 'hidden gems' category.

How they find these 'hidden gems' remains a mystery to me. But their choices are invariably good ones like they are at the Garrick.

It was at the Lauriston I saw one of my favourite amateur productions in 2006. Someone Who'll Watch Over Me by Frank McGuiness, gives you a flavour of what Terry Waite et al went through at the hands of the hostage takers wile it isn't a direct re-telling of the story. Tense and life affirming, this modern-day classic is ripe for revival and, featuring five-star performances, this was an amateur production only in name.

If I was to name all my personal favourites this book would doubtless turn into War and Peace. But Someone Who'll Watch Over Me is closely followed by Henry James's genuinely spooky ghost story, The Turn of The Screw staged at Altrincham Little Theatre. which I had the pleasure of reviewing as a fresh faced freelance in the 1980s. It was so tense in parts I actually felt like someone was sitting on my chest.

Altrincham Garrick also gave me something of an interview coup when Gareth Gwenlan came to Trafford. While the name might not be instantly recognisable to you, the chances are you will have heard of some of the TV classics he produced. Programmes like Only Fools and Horses, To The Manor Born and The Fall and Rise of Reginald Perrin are among the long list of hit shows that can be found on his CV. He spent a year as the Garrick's artistic director in the mid 60s.

As someone who spent many, many years interviewing people who largely making their living in front of the camera, it was really refreshing to meet someone who made their living behind it.

The Garrick's former Playhouse manager, Nev Roby, said Gwenlan used to live on a canal barge near to what is now Timperley tram station and recalled with fondness the legendary parties he hosted at his floating home.

I met Gareth when he visited Trafford as part of a trip to the then newly opened BBC centre at Salford Quays. He'd come north to shoot a pilot for a new comedy called The Pearly Gates, which saw the genial Welshman re-united with Only Fools and Horses star, David Jason, who he rated as one of the most gifted comedy actors he's worked with, along with Leonard Rossitter, who brought Perrin so memorably to life on the small screen and Penelope Keith, who he described as superb performer.

The borough also has a formidable reputation for producing top quality musicals and the Garrick has joined in on the act. Other groups include Sale and Altrincham Musical Theatre, Trafford Margaretians and Urmston Musical Theatre.

Professional actor Matthew Kelly is probably UMT's most famous graduate.

Returning to the subject of celebrity interviews, I also enjoyed chatting to pop princess Katie Melua, a refreshingly down to earth singer songwriter who, despite her stardom, prefers to socialise with her school friends rather than fellow celebs. I chatted to her prior to a gig at the Manchester Arena in 2008 and I was well and truly charmed. As well as being hugely talented, Melua is also stunningly beautiful. Unfortunately for me, we had to chat on the phone.

Dishing the dirt on celebrities was never in my remit. That said, I do remember annoying soap star Steve McFadden who plays Eastenders hard man Phil Mitchell in the popular soap. I suggested to him the programme was a bit, er, depressing at times.

Cue a withering look. "Twenty million people watch it every week," he replied.

Mc Fadden, who looks just as 'ard in real life, was at the press launch of Peter Pan at the Manchester Opera House. He played Captain Hook.

The late comedian Sean Lock, familiar to millions as one of the team captains on Channel 4's 8 Out Of 10 Cats Does Countdown particularly attracted my attention as it's not every day you get the chance to interview somebody who went through such a dramatic career change. Lock used to be a labourer so I suppose you could say he trained at the school of hard knocks.

I interviewed Lock in 2010 when he was about to bring his new stand-up show to The Lowry in Salford. The show featured a new approach to good old audience participation. Rather than have the punters cringe in their seats, the likeable Lock would read out a seat number and invite the person sitting in it to read out a letter and he would come up with a joke using that letter.

Personally, I liked the sound of this type of audience 'participation', so often a byword for humiliation. Lock has a laid-back manner and despite being one of the new breed of stand ups, has a lifelong admiration for old school greats like Tommy Cooper.

In 2015 I met the ice-skating legends Torvill and Dean as they were about to perform in their first ever panto, Cinderella, at the Opera House in Manchester.

The achieved international fame after performing what is now their legendary Bolero routine at the 1984 Olympics. They had reprised the iconic performance in Sarajevo a year earlier, to mark the 30th anniversary of their gold medal winning routine.

They both evidently relish a new challenge and Christopher was looking forward to bringing the children's classic to life on skates, armed with some brand-new choreography. Torvill and Dean, the archetypal golden couple who look like they've just stepped out of a fairy tale are as nice and as charming as I expected them to be, and I also liked the way Jayne leaned forward during my questions to make sure she understood everything that I said. A nice touch.

Personally, I've never been a fan of the pantomime. However, it doubtless plays a part in introducing children to the theatre and for that it's probably a good thing.

But the jokes make me cringe and the formula they follow is oh so tired. Oh yes it is!

Like Torvill and Dean, the magician Paul Daniels also made a good impression on me. I went into the Editor's office to do the interview with Daniels, who was bringing his one man show to Altrincham's Garrick Theatre. For some reason PD couldn't do the interview there and then so he asked me if he could ring me back the following morning. I suggested a time, he agreed, and the phone rang, on the dot. "I liked this, quite a lot," actually.

You could be cynical and say it was in his interests to call me back as he was promoting his own show. But it always feels good when someone goes the extra mile.

It was in the early 80s that I became politically aware and one of my favourite unofficial sports was Thatcher bashing, as practised by the multi-talented then comedy motormouth, Ben Elton. His lightning delivery and razor-sharp humour meant everything stopped in the Bowen household whenever he was on TV.

The thought of meeting the iconic writer and performer who I'd idolised as a teenager filled me with a mixture of excitement and dread. Would he turn out to be a miserable sod, like so many people involved in comedy turn out to be?

I shouldn't have worried. Elton, who was at the Palace Theatre in Manchester to promote the UK tour of the Queen musical, We Will Rock You, was as endearingly entertaining away from the big bright lights of showbusiness as he is while he's in the spotlight.

Elton, with his sparkly stage suit, was one of the architects of a comedy revolution. I'd grown up watching sitcoms that were largely safe, suburban, and inoffensive. But here we had a crop of very, very talented performers who tackled previously taboo subjects on stage and screen and didn't flinch when it came to give 'the establishment' a kicking.

In the autumn of 1982, a programme was aired on BBC2 that left viewers in no doubt that comedy was changing, and Ben Elton was one of its co-writers. The programme, of course, was The Young Ones, set in a filthy student house and featuring Ade Edmondson, later to become the hubby of the comedian Jennifer Saunders, as the sadistic and psychotic punk, Vivian.

As Vivian, he made me laugh until my sides hurt as he subjected his house mates, particularly Rik Mayall's character, to his own unique brand of slapstick sadism. He basically reprised the role nearly a decade later when he played a character who shared many of Vivian's 'unique' character traits in the equally hilarious, Bottom.

Ade's character was called Eddie Hitler and the show saw him once again playing opposite his Young Ones co-star, Rik Mayall.

A consummate comedy performer, he was taken from us far, far too soon. He died at the age of just 56.

Rik Mayall was especially brilliant as the unashamedly obnoxious Conservative MP Alan B'stard in another classic comedy, The New Statesman.

It was a real thrill then, to be given an opportunity to interview Ade when he was coming to The Lowry not as an actor, as a musician. He had formed a group called The Bad Shepherds who perform punk songs – with a Celtic twist. The real Ade Edmondson is, of course, nothing like the TV roles I still largely associate him with, even though a quick glance through his credits on imdb.com is living proof of his versatility.

In real life he's quiet and unassuming and refined and has an unforced charisma that makes it impossible to dislike him.

The most colourful character I interviewed came early on in my career was Cynthia Payne, before she appeared at the Bowdon Rooms in Bowdon, near Altrincham. A former brothel keeper in London, Payne spoke of her previous profession in a very entertaining and insightful way. Or in the words of the late, great Kenny Everett's comic creation Cupid Stunt, it was all done "in the best possible taste."

Cynthia, who had a difficult start in life, ran a brothel in London which was memorably raided by police in the late 70's. Some of her clients had disabilities and she recalled them, armed with their walking sticks, and walking frames, trying to flee the scene and falling into hedgerows and over walls as they did so.

My interview with the colourful Cynthia is one of my favourites and recalling it certainly brought a smile to my face.

And Payne's colourful life loosely inspired two of my favourite films, Wish You Were Here and Personal Services, the latter starring Julie Walters, an actress who was born to be funny.

But Cynthia denied the claims she ever used the playful insult 'up your bum' in Wish You Were Here. She was played by the actress Emily Lloyd.

I interviewed Emily's dad, the late Roger Lloyd Pack, twice at the Royal Exchange and found him very laid back and very refined. An actor of great versatility, he is probably best remembered for playing Trigger, the lovably dim-witted road sweeper in the BBC sitcom, Only Fools and Horses.

Roger, like me, had a deep-seated affection for Trigger – so much so we both agreed he was one of the funniest sitcom characters ever. Who can forget the way 'Trig' repeatedly got Rodney's name wrong and called him Dave or his propensity for getting the wrong end of the stick, which this clueless character turned into an art form.

But Tony Robinson's amiable buffoon Baldrick from the classic sitcom Blackadder, runs Trigger a very close second. He appeared alongside Rowan Atkinson in the hugely popular sitcom, Blackadder. A strong cast also included Miranda Richardson as a spoilt brat of a Queen Elizabeth and Stephen Fry as the grovelling, sycophantic courtier, Lord Melchett.

Baldrick had many a 'cunning plan' in the show – but none of them ever came off.

I met Tony when he attended an environmental awards ceremony in Trafford in 2005 amid rumours there were plans for a fifth Blackadder series set in the 'Swinging Sixties.' Tony put the show's success down to the clever and witty scripts that made this sideways look at history so popular and the fact the classic sitcom had the brainless Baldrick at the centre of it.

While he might have been making us laugh for decades in Blackadder, there is one subject that Tony is deadly serious about. The environment. He's spoken at conferences organised by Greenpeace, Friends of the Earth and the government's environmental watchdog, the Environment Agency.

I tend to think of recycling as something new. But Tony insists it isn't and believes the future is not pre-ordained and insisted we can shape it for the benefit of future generations.

Returning to the theatre, I've often wondered what an actor or an actress has to do to get a standing ovation these days. I've sat through many, many productions and been completely baffled when an audience remains seated by the time of the curtain call.

Now I know us critics are supposed to remain detached and all that. But there's something magical and uplifting when you're a part of a spontaneous outpouring of emotion, isn't there?

Standing ovations tend to come at the end of performances. Unless your name is Sir Roger Moore of course. The James Bond star actually brought the audience to its feet *before* he said a word and shared stories from his glittering showbiz career when he appeared at The Lowry in 2013.

My son James, then 13, was hooked on all things 007 and like me said he thought he was dreaming as he saw the showbiz legend in the flesh.

Sir Roger unlocked a treasure trove of tales from a career that began with him as a jobbing actor, staying in digs that were a world away from the luxurious lifestyle enjoyed by the world's most famous secret agent.

This was followed by a Q&A with the audience, and I was impressed by the way this star of the big screen came across, as an un-affected, affable man of the people. The afternoon ended on an emotional note, as Roger talked passionately about his work with the children's charity, UNICEF.

While I was grateful for the review tickets provided by the Lowry press team which had elevated me to super Dad status with James, I would have killed for an interview with Moore.

But it was an afternoon the both of us never did forget.

The re-opening of The Bowdon Rooms as The Cinnamon Club gave a much-needed boost to the live music scene in Trafford and it soon became a big draw for fans of jazz and soul from Greater Manchester and beyond.

Neil Hughes, its former owner, organised some fantastic interviews with acts who were appearing there, including one with Clare Teal. Imagine, if you can, someone who combines the comedic warmth of a Victoria Wood with a vocal range that is simply breath taking. It has to be heard to be believed.

Neil has since sold up and the venue has become The Bowdon Rooms once again. But, at the time of writing, the house lights are temporarily turned off due to the Coronavirus pandemic.

Speaking of key figures from the world of jazz, I had the pleasure of interviewing jazz legend Cleo Laine, and I was well and truly charmed by a lady whose speaking voice is just as sultry as her singing voice. Cleo appeared at the Cinnamon Club in Altrincham and told me she has a 400-seat music venue, The Stables, in the grounds of her home in Buckinghamshire.

The aim of the venue, which the Tony award winning singer opened with her husband John was to give a platform to new musical talent. It also hosted gigs by acts who need no introduction, like Steve Harley and Cockney Rebel.

How the other half live, eh?

I interviewed this jazz legend before she appeared at the Cinnamon Club in 2005. The interview also appeared in Lifestyle magazine; a publication set up by the Messenger to compete with Cheshire Life.

When she won her jazz Grammy in 1985, Cleo received a congratulatory bunch of flowers from jazz queen Ella Fitzgerald, no less. At the end of the interview Cleo asked me very politely what my disability is and seemed very impressed when I told her I had cerebral palsy.

Staying with matters musical, my dad still has a copy of David Soul's album which I bought after becoming hooked on the American TV cop show in which he starred, the unforgettable Starsky and Hutch.

I came across this TV classic when I was channel flicking at home one evening and I remember it as a programme everyone talked about in the playground on Monday mornings. If you'd missed it, you never admitted it, for fear of being vilified by your mates.

Soul played Detective Ken 'Hutch' Hutchinson opposite the more volatile but hugely charismatic Paul Michael Glaser. I was so obsessed with this programme my mum's best friend Beryl knitted me a cream coloured Starsky style cardigan.

In 2006 I had chance to interview David Soul when he was about to appear as the silent movie mogul Mack Stennett in Mack and Mabel at Manchester's Palace Theatre. To say I was excited at the prospect of spending time with one of my teen idols was understatement of the year even if it was only for the standard 15 minutes.

After interviewing Soul for about two minutes, it became apparent his days of chasing the bad guys through the mean streets of Bay City were long, long behind him. He was a revelation as Stennett and so was his former crime fighting partner, Paul Michael Glaser who played Tevye, the deposed patriarch, in the classic musical Fiddler On The Roof at The Lowry in 2013. Unfortunately, PMG didn't do any interviews, which was a pity.

In 2006 the Royal Exchange Theatre celebrated its 30th birthday with a production of Ma Rainey's Black Bottom, by August Wilson. Personally, I felt *my* birthday had come early because the play about the blues icon starred one Antonio Fargas, known to millions of Starsky and Hutch fans as that cool dude Huggy Bear, the cops' eyes and ears on the street.

So, I *finally* got to interview someone from one of my favourite all-time TV shows in the flesh. Tall and refined, Antonio was to play Toledo, the piano player in Ma Rainey's band in a piece set in 1927 against the backdrop of the appalling racism suffered by black people in the United States.

I was intrigued, as doubtless many theatregoers were by the prospect of seeing an actor so inextricably linked with a classic role try something new.

He was excellent of course and told me he was grateful for the career boost appearing in Starsky and Hutch gave him, particularly in the UK.

I can remember pestering my dad to buy a Ford Gran Torino, the car used by Starsky and Hutch as they screeched around the mean streets of Bay City, chasing the bad guys.

This programme, which was ultimately ruined when the anti-violence brigade got their meddling mitts on it, was hailed as ground-breaking by Fargas.

I hated the anti-violence on TV mob epitomised by the prim and proper Mary Whitehouse. Imagine that, a show in which two policemen spend their time chasing bad guys having violence in it? Shock horror.

If it's part of the story, keep it in there. If you don't like it, turn your bloody TV off.

Meeting Fargas was one of those occasions when the worlds of stage and screen collide, like the time I interviewed Roger Lloyd Pack when he appeared at the Royal Exchange.

Gavin and Stacey star Joanna Page was at the RET in 2011 to appear as Sybil Thorndike in Noel Coward's romantic comedy, Private Lives.

Despite the clipped, terribly English tone of Coward's piece, Page said it isn't that far removed from the way in which couple's interact with each other today.

The pretty Welsh actress delayed her lunch to wax lyrical about her role in Noel Coward's play.

But, like Roger Lloyd Pack, Joanna will be forever Stacey in the BBC's classic romantic comedy. She recalled being wowed by the script written by James Corden and Ruth Jones when she saw it for the first time.

A must for fans of gentle, beautifully observed comedy, the programme, a contemporary classic in my opinion, saw Joanna play opposite Matthew Horne in the lead roles. The couple were determined to make their relationship work despite the distance between them. Gavin was an Essex boy and Stacey hailed from South Wales.

Just in case you're wondering, Joanna is just as broad in real life as she is in Gavin and Stacey. Unlike her co-star and the sitcom's co-creator Ruth Jones, who speaks with hardly a trace of a Welsh accent whenever she's interviewed.

While Joanna was very open to the idea of working with Corden and Jones on future projects they had scripted, she was also receptive to the idea of playing a character who was more difficult to like than Stacey.

She told me her husband thought she was more than capable of playing formidable and feisty and while I found Joanna very friendly and easy to warm to, I was in no doubt I was in the company of someone who was more than capable of looking after herself.

I really enjoyed Gavin and Stacey. There are occasions when acting is so good, be it on stage or screen, you actually forget you're watching actors.

The episode in which Stacey's uncle Bryn, played so brilliantly by Rob Brydon, tries so hard to be cool and trendy and down with the young people when he's trying to organise Gavin's stag do was especially memorable and featured Brydon at his comic best.

While the comedy in Gavin and Stacey is gentle and inoffensive, I found comedian Roy 'Chubby' Brown was still courting controversy when I interviewed him in 2015. The infamous stand up was bringing his show, Sex, Drugs and Sausage Rolls to the Garrick Theatre in Altrincham.

I was intrigued by the prospect of spending some time with a man who I'd always thought all subjects for him were fair game when it came to comedy.

But even he won't make fun of certain things. There *are* certain subjects that are off limits, like making fun of sick or disabled children, according to the veteran stand up who was showing no signs of mellowing even though he'd recently turned 70.

One thing that has always intrigued me is the suit he wears on stage which is actually made from beer towels.

This sartorial quirk is a nod back to the late 60s when he was booked for stag dos and, as well as spitting at him, some members of the audience also threw beer over him.

Maybe that's what they mean by suffering for your art.

I didn't get to see the show and to make up my own mind about just how controversial his act is, which was a pity.

When we spoke, he promised the audience a mix of material that included current affairs and an attempt to provide a much-needed antidote to the general doom and gloom.

Personally, I've never made my mind up about controversial stand ups like Roy Chubby Brown. To me they belong in a different era.

Some people might say I'm a hypocrite because one of my favourite comedians happens to be Frankie Boyle who is notorious for pushing the comic boundaries. But I do tune in to his TV shows, excited by the prospect of what he's going to say next.

Sex, Drugs and Sausage Rolls came to Trafford with a sort of health warning. If easily offended – please stay away.

Roy in real life is as far removed from his stage persona as you could possibly get, as many comedians are.

I've always loved music and can recall spending all my pocket money on Mott the Hoople's single, All the Young Dudes when I was just six years old.

My favourite band is The Killers and I enjoy nothing better than furthering my musical education by listening to the new music station 6Music or watching Later with Jools Holland's show on BBC2.

I met photographer Mick Rock – great surname for a guy in his line of work – when an exhibition of his work was put on at Urbis in Manchester in 2005. Rock, sporting shades and a denim jacket, certainly looked the part and his career, which then spanned more than 40 years, included working with a true pop genius, the late, great David Bowie.

Rock described the boy from Brixton as bright and articulate and praised the star, whose long and illustrious career was just starting back then, for the way he coped with fame.

He's also worked with The Killers, who I first discovered on 6Music. So, I was very, very jealous of the man behind the shades.

My interviews with top musicians also included Tim Booth from James who, I discovered actually has a connection with Trafford. He lived in Dunham Massey, the picture postcard village just outside Altrincham. He lived there for three years.

It fascinated me to think me and my best friend San – who many people have assumed over the years that we were going out – saw James play at a music festival in Platt Fields in Manchester in the mid-80s. The 'mosh' pit at the front of the stage contained no more than around 20 diehard fans. James have since evolved into a global supergroup.

By the way, is everyone aware that the band's superficially anthem like, uplifting hit Sit Down is actually about somebody living with mental illness?

There's a nugget of trivia with which to impress your friends at dinner parties.

Boy George, ex-lead singer of 80's band, Culture Club was at The Lowry to promote what was then his new musical, Taboo in 2003. Intelligent, warm, witty, and charismatic, this colourful character, and I use the phrase in both senses of the word, was one of my favourite interviews with people from the world of pop.

George would be the perfect dinner guest and even I who was rationed to just a 15-minute conversation with him was well and truly captivated.

In short, he's great company.

Then there was Peter Hook from New Order, a musician known to have a great sense of humour. I managed to make him laugh at the start of our chat. "How long have we got for the interview," I asked. "Depends how good your questions are," he said. "Bloody brilliant," I replied. Cue hysterics from Hooky.

Writing about music in terms of CD reviews is something I've always struggled with and while I was required to do them now and again, I was quite happy to let this perk of the job be handled by other reporters. I found reviewing CDs as easy as solving a Maths problem that was put before me when I was at school. I remember recently reading a review of The Killers' new album, Exploding the Mirage in The Guardian and being totally in awe of the person who had written it. Why I suffer this mental block after being a fan of pop music since the early 70s is a mystery to me.

But not all my memorable interviews were rooted in the world of celebrity. For instance, there was my visit to Styal Women's Prison to talk to some of the inmates about an arts project they were involved in. That experience was as frightening as it was illuminating. Don't get me wrong – it wasn't being in the women's company that frightened me – they were politeness personified – it was the fact that all our movements around the site, myself and the photographer, were dictated by a prison officer brandishing a set of keys. It felt decidedly odd, even though I was aware we would soon be leaving HMP Styal.

Then there were the two fascinating features I wrote about the work of Trafford Community Drugs Team. It was the most revealing of experiences and actually included my first ever meeting with a drug user which shattered any preconceptions I'd ever held about such people.

This guy was articulate, intelligent, and perceptive and he never stopped wondering how different his life could have been had he taken a different path. I found covering such social issues a really stimulating experience and I do hope this man who was brave enough to tell me his story was actually able to turn his life around.

As someone who has 'first hand' experience of what it feels like to be discriminated against I felt delighted when the job gave me the opportunity to tell the story of those people who were going through a similar thing.

I hate discrimination in all its forms. Whether it's on the grounds of race, gender, disability, or sexual orientation. It just doesn't sit well with me at all. In 2003 I met Samantha Valentine, a transsexual from Sale who had suffered appalling treatment at the hands of certain members of the public.

This even included having a car driven at her. What planet are these people on? This radical surgery isn't something you go through on a whim and Samantha didn't skimp on the details when telling me about the post op agony she'd had to endure. After the piece was printed, she sent me a heartfelt thank you letter and details of the incidents of public support she'd been showered with since we printed the story.

There was also my interview with Stanley Hyman, the butcher from Bowdon who was retiring. It made a decent piece, Stanley and I had a pleasant chat and he told me the family business, a kosher butchers, was set up by his grandfather who came to this country on board one of the most iconic ships of the 20th century, The Titanic.

Naturally, I was very disappointed when Stanley told me he never spoke about his experience. Then he brought out a brown envelope which had been sent to him by a relative in America. Inside was an interview he'd given to one of the papers over there in which he recalled the sinking of the famous vessel so vividly I actually felt I was there.

So, I got two stories after visiting Mr Hyman. With hindsight, we should have held the second one over until some significant anniversary to mark the sinking of this supposedly unsinkable ship. However, I was anxious for it not to fall into the hands of another newspaper, so I persuaded the Editor to run it sooner rather than later.

During my time at the Messenger, I worked hard on creating a Leisure section that was a healthy mix of theatre and film reviews and celebrity interviews. While I worked hard on developing my own writing style, I have always been influenced by the way they cover the arts scene in The Guardian. The journalists on that particular publication write in a way that's intelligent, witty, clever, readable and insightful, always treating their readers as if they have something between their ears.

In terms of live theatre, I could spend two or three nights a week reviewing plays and shows in Trafford and Manchester. As a critic of both theatre and film I've always been guided by the following three rules when reviewing – what is the play or show about, what were the most memorable aspects of it and is it worth people spending their hard earned money on to go and see it.

I started reviewing films because I felt it gave the Leisure section a better balance in terms of content and I didn't want it to be 'top heavy' with theatre reviews and previews. This meant I wouldn't eat my tea until around 9pm some nights, having gone straight to the cinema from the office. But at least I was doing something I enjoyed.

While I could easily have filled the space with generic copy, I wanted the Leisure section to have its own identity and not contain generic articles that could be read by our readers anywhere. And besides, the cinema is a place where magic happens and is hugely popular with people of all ages. When I go, I want to leave this often-humdrum world of ours behind sometimes and don't really care if a movie is far-fetched or not.

I can remember watching a James Bond film with Sean Connery and he was kissing and canoodling with a drop-dead gorgeous Bond girl. "I want to be a spy when I grow up," I said. My dad laughed uncontrollably. "It's not really like that – or else everyone would be joining up," he said.

While I hate those catty critics who slate something for the sake of it there are aspects of the performing arts I hate with a passion. I've tried. Honestly, I have. But I hate with a passion the works of Gilbert and Sullivan. Their jaunty scores and the ridiculous word play of their lyrics just leave me cold. If hell does exist, the theatres will only show G&S on a loop, 24 hours a day.

But The Mikado is bearable – just.

I saw my first play in 1982 and it happened purely by accident. My mum and dad were off to the Royal Exchange in Manchester with two good friends of theirs and mum had to pull out as she was in hospital. Being a teenager – I was 17 at the time – I didn't want to go. Hating anything that was out of my comfort zone, part of every teen's job description, some might say.

The play we saw was The Nerd, a side-splitting comedy about two very different characters and it made my sides ache with laughter. It was a big deal for the Exchange too – being the European premiere of Larry Shue's play.

As a theatre critic I've never set myself up as a barometer of good taste and I hope I've never come across as being that arrogant in my writing. Hopefully I've persuaded people to try new things when it comes to live theatre.

I felt very flattered when a member of staff at Altrincham Garrick actually told me their patrons made their choices based on what I say in my reviews.

Even when I was surrounded by an office full of people, I've always found writing a very lonely occupation because it's hard to imagine someone sitting down and actually reading what you've written over their early morning cuppa or after their evening meal.

Why do I enjoy trips to the theatre so much? It can be entertaining and educational and spring surprises on you. I also enjoy sharing the experience with an audience and live theatre has an immediacy that you just don't get with most TV dramas. You can't just switch off a play or a show.

It's also an art form that can be performed pretty much anywhere – I've even seen productions performed in a converted car ferry courtesy of Walk the Plank when their home was on the Manchester Ship Canal.

I even saw a performance of Romeo and Juliet at Manchester's stunning Victoria Baths. Minus the water of course!

My favourite playwrights are William Shakespeare, Arthur Miller, Harold Pinter and Alan Bennett. When it comes to musicals, I'm something of a Steven Sondheim nut. His show Company is my favourite, an uplifting musical in which a group of friends try to get one of their number married off.

I saw it at the old Library Theatre and left feeling really uplifted and entertained.

My career at the SAM also saw me rubbing shoulders with Royalty. Well, sort of. When a royal visit takes place us mere mortals aren't allowed to speak to the visitor unless you're invited to do so. I remember covering a visit by Prince Charles to Altrincham Grammar School for Girls in 2003. On a tour of the school, HRH watched one of the lessons in progress and the teacher singled out one of the pupils and asked her to explain what the class was studying.

The poor girl died of embarrassment, her face giving us that 'ground please swallow me up' look. This prompted the prince to turn to her and say "Jolly bad luck, isn't it?" She relaxed on the spot and duly answered her teacher's question.

The school, which began its academic life as Altrincham County High School for Girls, also has a Royal connection. Its first headmistress, Miss Mary Howes Smith, who took up her post in 1910, was a tutor to the Princess Royal. She taught HRH History and English Literature respectively.

I went on a guided tour of Prince Charles's former Navy ship, HMS Bronington, when it was temporarily moored on the Manchester Ship Canal. What struck me as we roamed the Bronington was how cramped the living conditions were. Even the Prince, who captained the vessel for a time, slept in a tiny cabin in which you couldn't swing a cat.

What also struck me was just how fit the Royal Navy sailors must be as many parts of the vessel could only be reached using ladders that were scary in terms of their size.

Then there was Prince Philip's visit to Trafford Park. Not being able to take notes meant I would sometimes speak into my tape recorder to have a record of what had taken place. I remember doing this on the quayside and briefly attracting the attention of one of HRH's bodyguards who may have thought I was about to whip out a gun or something!

Don't get me wrong, I'm not a royalist by any stretch of the imagination. But the way Prince Charles interacted with those he met on his visit to Altrincham certainly changed my impression of him and I believe no Government, regardless of its political complexion, would dare get rid of them.

But a slimmed down version of the Monarchy is very, very appealing.

After family and the theatre, the third biggest love of my life has been Manchester City FC. It was my uncle who first made me aware of the Blues when I was a tot and he would jump around the living room like a mad thing whenever Francis Lee scored a goal, screaming out his name like a boy possessed.

For decades, following the Blues was certainly a labour of love and the lowest point came when we were relegated to the Third Division, now Division One, in the 90's.

But even when City were awful, the humour of the fans on the Maine Road terraces was worth the ticket money on its own.

I can remember going to watch City's second string play a friendly at Altrincham FC. There were two City fans standing near me who were so funny my sides ached by the time I left the ground. A particular target of theirs was one of our strikers, Gareth Taylor, who was subject to some good, humoured jibes.

Not all Blues fans laughed when the team was laughable. I remember a guy sitting near me at Maine Road when we were playing Tranmere Rovers and the team from the Wirral had just equalised to make it 1-1. "This is complete shite," he screamed at the top of his voice. I wouldn't have minded – but he was the manager!

I jest, of course.

We were nothing like the force we are today, thanks to the deep pockets of our owner, Sheikh Mansour. Most of my family are Reds. However, at no point did I ever consider jumping ship and switching my allegiance to United, even when the club was winning every trophy in sight.

Being a reporter on the Messenger meant I was able to meet several Man City icons, including Mike Summerbee, the flying winger from the legendary 60's/70's side. I went to interview 'Buzzer' as we Blues call him, for our Lifestyle magazine.

It was a sort of profile piece and I remained very professional and resisted the temptation to ask him for a kick about before we left. There was a football and a mini net on his back lawn which his grandchildren used to play with. I am too young to really remember 'Buzzer' from his playing days and I wanted to see if he still 'had it.'

Mike has an entire room in his house given over to Man City memorabilia.

I imagine this Blues icon was great fun in the dressing room. Just before we left, he received a phone call from former teammate Francis Lee and joked how we'd made him pose for photos wearing just his jockstrap!

But I was too young to remember that great Man City side of the 60s and 70s. I grew up idolising the team featuring striker Denis Tueart who entered club folklore after he scored that legendary overhead kick that won the Blues the League Cup back in 1976.

It was a huge thrill when I got to interview one of my sporting idols and even better that he lived at the time in Trafford.

The interview came about thanks to my cleaner at the time, Vivian, who knew him. Or something like that.

When it came to an interview, the ex-England star was mysteriously reticent at first, citing bad experiences he had in the past with the tabloid press which operate in a totally different world to the world of the Messenger. But we ended up having a good interview with DT happy to answer all my questions with the exception of the one about former City chairman Peter Swales.

Other leading figures from the world of sport I've met was the former snooker world champion Shaun Murphy who used to practice at Sale Conservative Club on a table costing nearly as much as my whole year's salary.

The promotions company founded by boxing legend Ricky 'The Hitman' Hatton actually hosted a fight featuring Ricky's little brother Matthew at Altrincham Leisure Centre in 2009.

To interview him, I went along with our photographer to his gym where he was in the middle of a training session, and it has to be one of the scariest things I've ever seen.

Hatton, who isn't the tallest of fighters, delivered punches to his trainer's pads that were so powerful and deadly in their accuracy he nearly knocked the guy off his feet.

And we're talking about a trainer who was tall and lean and pure muscle.

I have to say I've never really been a fan of boxing because of the health risks associated with the sport.

But even I have to say watching the trainer's pads get such a pounding from a top athlete like 'The Hitman' was one of the most impressive spectacles I've ever seen.

Outside the ring, Ricky's like a different person – quiet and considered. It was like someone had flicked a switch and turned his aggression off.

There isn't a hint of sibling rivalry between Ricky and Matthew. The Hitman said while they train together their friendship exists outside the gym and spoke of his pride in relation to Matthew's progress in the sport.

When I met Hatton, he was about to face what he regarded as one of the toughest challenges of his career to date in the shape of Manny Pacquaio.

Rather you than me, Manny.

I also found out about The Hitman's Trafford connections in so far as he used to train at Sale West ABC when he was growing up.

While Ricky and I are of a similar size, I felt like a small boy when I stood next to the Olympic great Sir Steve Redgrave when he visited Flixton Girls School in 2015. Sir Steve is 6ft 5in tall, exactly a foot taller than little old me who definitely gets his height from mum's side of the family.

The athlete, whose won multiple gold medals in rowing at various Olympics, was in north Trafford to recognise the success of the Sporting Promise programme which was set up to encourage more young people to take up sport.

Sir Steve, who holds the title of Britain's most decorated Olympian – having won five gold medals at successive competitions – said taking part isn't just about finding the next Olympic champion. Getting involved can improve fitness and verbal communication and competitive skills that young people can carry over into the world of work.

Then there were the series of pieces I wrote about Chapel Street in Altrincham. It was dubbed the 'bravest little street in England' by King George V after 161 men from 61 houses signed up to fight for their country in the First World War.

My great granddad, Hugh Hennerley, was among them. The very thought he, my own flesh and blood, was involved in such a thing filled me with great pride.

The men involved signed up for the Cheshire Regiment – a regiment with a king and illustrious history that includes serving in The Boer War.

But my family involvement didn't end there. My second cousin, Peter Hennerley, was instrumental in getting a plaque put up to mark the location of the long-demolished street. He also campaigned tirelessly for a lasting memorial to these brave souls which now stands in Staffordshire.

My story was sold to The Daily Mail. Ah well, beggars can't be choosers.

When I was growing up, I was a huge, huge fan of Echo and the Bunnymen and I remember playing their tapes to death. I even went as far as buying several second-hand overcoats and numerous cheque shirts which became the unofficial uniform of fans of the band.

Such clobber was generally picked up on frequent trips to Affleck's Palace in the 80s, then an emporium of all things alternative. If you're the type of person who hates pushy shopkeepers Affleck's was the place to go because the shopkeepers, helpful as always if you need it, gave off a refreshing air of utter indifference as to whether you bought anything or not.

I loved that and I equally loved my trip to Bilko's, a shop on the ground floor of Affleck's which sold clothes with a retro, 50's feel to them.

Back to Echo and the Bunnymen. I even got to interview Will Sergeant, the band's bassist who revealed a passion for painting and actually asked me what my favourite album by them was and seemed genuinely interested in my answer, which was nice. I think I said Porcupine.

Since playing that again I've changed my opinion to one of their later releases, Ocean Rain. How fickle us pop fans are.

In October 2015 I was delighted to get a press ticket to watch an intimate gig at the Waterside Arts Centre in Sale featuring Ian McCulloch, lead singer of the afore mentioned indie giants.

Around four weeks later I was made redundant.

While the RADAR journalism training bursaries were a great idea, I never encountered any other reporters with disabilities. I tried to find out how many disabled people had gone on to get jobs as a result of the bursary scheme when I was researching this book. But I was told by someone at the organisation, which has since undergone a name change, that records didn't go back that far, which made me feel very old.

My advice to budding journalists is be determined, don't be put off and get as much of your work published as possible. If you do this, you'll eventually be known for your writing and not the fact you happen to be disabled.

It's also important to develop your own writing style and while it's ok to be influenced by other publications – I admire the intelligent and yet very readable style of The Guardian – don't try mimicking it. Also, resist the temptation to throw in big words. I can remember reading an article in The Independent and my reading of the piece came to a shuddering halt when I came across a word I didn't understand.

Accuracy is also very important because a mistake can, if serious, result in your employers being sued. I did go through a phase of making a number of mistakes when my marriage was failing, and it actually saw me get a written warning from my Editor. So, I faced losing the job I'd worked doubly hard to get.

They say you should leave your problems at the office door. But sometimes that's easier said than done.

Also check how names are spelt. For instance, I've come across three different spellings of Claire – Claire, Clare, and Clair. While getting somebody's name wrong is hardly a hanging offence it makes you the reporter look unprofessional and undermines the credibility of your story or article when it appears in print. Readers may think if he can't get the person's bloody name right, what other mistakes has he made?

You also need to be able to interview all sorts of different people. When I was interviewing children, I always found it a real challenge most of the time – and it wasn't because they struggled to understand me. I could pose what I thought was a decent question only for it to be greeted by a one-word answer!

On the other hand, there are many kids who are impressively articulate, sometimes with a little prompting from a parent or teacher.

And resist the temptation to ask the same questions. I found myself falling into this trap briefly when I used to write my People profile column because I was acutely aware of the amount of space I had in the paper each week. Writing to a formula can become very boring for the reader. I also changed the way I wrote my reviews the more experienced I became because I didn't want them to become predictable either.

While the pay in journalism isn't as good as it is in other professions it's an interesting and fascinating job that brings you into contact with a wide variety of people who generally have an interesting story to tell. Had I become a glorified pen pusher stuck in some anonymous office I would have been bored to tears.

But had I been born able bodied I probably would have opted for a very different profession. Pilot. But as the housemate I fancied to death in my student house once pointed out, I am more orientated towards English anyway, so it was probably inevitable that I ended up doing something creative.

If you're lucky enough to get a place on the NCTJ course, you'll spend most of your time writing news stories and while it never came naturally to me it was a skill I was able to master. But I was lucky enough to work alongside Chris Griffin, our senior reporter for many years and I was able to bounce ideas off him relating to news stories.

I wrote them of course. I just used Chris, whose temperament would make him ideal material for the teaching profession, as a sort of sounding board.

A placid bloke with the patience of a saint, Chris also never stopped encouraging me to carry on trying to get into journalism even when I was feeling frustrated by my lack of success. Most of our meetings took place after a boozy night in Manchester after stumbling off the last train.

Nor is journalism the sort of job to go into if you're the type of person who likes to be praised for their work or receive a "thank you" for a piece you've written or the way you've written it.

Nuala, our publisher, spent time at our office though and seemed generally impressed after I told her of the celebrity interviews I'd secured for Lifestyle magazine, which was, after all, her baby. With the exception of the 'at home with' pieces I had to write and their emphasis on interior design, which bores me rigid, I loved Lifestyle because it gave me much more space for celebrity interviews than the paper ever did.

Had I been able-bodied I would have liked to have been a social affairs correspondent for the BBC because I find this field of journalism particularly fascinating.

Without wanting to label myself as some sort of crusader, my first opportunity to do just that came when the Messenger group launched Xtra, a pull-out supplement full of cinema reviews, theatre reviews and stories that covered arts and leisure activities in Manchester city centre and the areas covered by our sister papers.

It saw journalists from across our group sharing stories and articles and for me it was a perfect outlet for my writing talents.

I wrote about Manchester's vibrant gay village in the mid-90s. The area, previously a seedy, commercial wasteland, had rapidly become a magnet for partygoers and the number of businesses that had sprung up over the years had given it a much-needed economic shot in the arm.

So, a tour of the area was booked and Chris Payne, who I sort of knew from my City Life days, was my unofficial tour guide. It's a really cool place and has been dubbed Manchester's answer to Amsterdam.

Chris used to edit the gay section in City Life and said a tour of this budding area wouldn't be complete without a trip to Clonezone. The shop, which still holds the title of the world's largest gay business, sells the sort of stuff you wouldn't usually find on the high street, like gay erotica and fetish wear!

Setting up the photo of Ian, who ran the shop at the time, involved a certain amount of discretion, bearing in mind the racy nature of some of his stock!

But Colin, one of our photographers at the time, certainly rose to the challenge.

I also wrote a piece on The Village charity and the terrific work it was doing to raise funds for AIDS research.

Going into journalism also increases your chances of working with people who are fun and entertaining, and I got on like a house on fire with the majority of my colleagues. There were a couple who I felt like putting out the bunting when they left. But they were the exception, rather than the rule.

One of the most memorable was definitely Maggie, a lovely mixed-race lady who had been adopted and raised in The Isle of Wight. Maggie had personality coming out of her ears, she was funny, outgoing, and got my humour. I remember having a conversation with her about disability and her saying to me after I'd had a rant: "Not everyone deliberately goes out to be nasty, Rick – some people just don't know how to react."

It's really important not to be a catty critic when reviewing films or anything else. I find it very childish and boring when journalists slate a play or a show for the sake of it.

A former colleague of mine took great delight in telling me once how he'd reviewed an amateur theatre production and absolutely slated it which I thought was very nasty indeed, especially when many unpaid actors and actresses who go to a rehearsal after doing a full day's work.

If I saw an amateur play or show featuring someone in the cast who couldn't act their way out of a paper bag, I just wouldn't mention them in my review.

Also, amateur theatre in Trafford allows people to enjoy top quality entertainment on their doorstep and not everyone has the money or the inclination to go into Manchester to watch a professional play or show.

Or to put it another way, amateur theatres provide a valuable service to the communities they are a part of.

While I was at the Messenger, I also wrote a weekly people profile column, and I can remember being totally captivated when meeting Georgie Ellis. The daughter of the last woman to be hanged in this country, Georgie lived in Hale and was in no doubt her mother didn't deserve to die for the murder of her abusive lover, David Blakely.

I also interviewed a lady from Sale who ran the women's section at Risley Remand Centre. She'd retired and had written a book about her challenging working life. She'd never forgotten the time one of the world's most notorious criminals, spent time at Risley before being transferred to another prison. This was after the evil Hindley had supposedly embraced Christianity. But my interviewee said she would not have trusted her as far as she could have thrown her.

Some interviews invariably cover subjects you'll know little about. My knowledge of cooking, which doesn't extend to knowing which button to press on the microwave and I haven't really cooked anything for anybody else since my student days.

Jay Rayner, food critic and son of the veteran TV presenter Claire Rayner, brought his one man show to the Waterside Arts Centre in 2015 in which he served up an evening of culinary horrors highlighting the worst dining experiences he's ever had.

The good news is that none of the restaurants Jay mentioned were in the north - they were all in London. Some were abroad.

Jay recalled a meal he had in Paris with his wife, washed down with two glasses of wine that cost £660. It's enough to drive you to drink.

In his show he would say the north fared well when it came to serving good food that was also good value and the worst offenders were, in his experience, in the capital.

Another memorable assignment to fall into my lap came courtesy of ex-BBC war reporter Martin Bell, whose famous white suit was featured in a 2011 exhibition at the Imperial War Museum North in Trafford Park. The exhibition was called War Correspondent: Reporting Under Fire Since 1914.

The former MP, put to bed forever the myth that when a country is at war it's taking place everywhere in the particular war zone 24/7.

This revelation conjured up memories of a conversation with former Messenger colleague Steve Edwards who travelled with an aid convoy to help civilians caught up in the conflict in the former Yugoslavia.

Steve said he could go for a morning coffee at a café and be served by a man who was a waiter in the morning and a soldier in the afternoon.

The Imperial War Museum North, which hosted the exhibition, is well worth a visit as it gives conflict a human face and concentrates on the heartache rather than the hardware.

Interviewing Martin Bell opened up a whole new world for me and what struck me was how matter of fact he is when it comes to talking about life on the front line.

Bell even said there were some cases when fighters would play to the camera by firing shots in the air and chanting slogans.

Kate Adie OBE, the former BBC war correspondent, also gave me an interesting and insightful interview when she came to Dunham Massey Hall near Altrincham in 2014. Adie was in Trafford to open Sanctuary from The Trenches, an exhibition that gave a fascinating insight into the role of the Hall in treating wounded British soldiers during the First World War.

She said many of the 'Tommies' had never slept in a bed before coming to Dunham and this made me feel rather sad.

Dunham Massey Hall was adapted to incorporate a range of facilities during the Great War and these facilities even included an operating theatre. It was home to the Earls of Stamford until the death of the last Earl, Roger Grey, in 1976.

The Hall is now run by The National Trust. The grand old houses really fire my imagination and I find myself wandering from room to room, imagining what life was like in years gone by.

When I first saw her, I thought Kate looked rather fierce and unapproachable. But a warmer and friendlier person I couldn't have wished for. The ex-war correspondent brought us news stories from the world's most notorious troubled spots, including the scene of the Tianemen Square massacre in China.

She said the job both shook and restored her faith in human nature.

Inevitably there were interviews I couldn't get, like pop genius David Bowie. I saw Bowie at Maine

Road in 1990 and have always been captivated by the late star's ability to reinvent himself.

I've always found the boy from Brixton fascinating and the way he was constantly creative, always pushing boundaries and always trying something new right up until the very end of his life and career.

He also appears to have been a very decent person. After watching a series of documentaries about him on BBC4 there wasn't a single interview that featured anyone saying anything derogatory about the 'thin white Duke.'

I also admire David Bowie for his unassuming, approachable, and refreshingly honest nature. Rest in peace, DB.

Likewise, the comedian Paul Merton was equally elusive, despite me putting in so many requests to his agent it could have been construed as harassment!

I've also been a fan of the band The Human League for decades now, from their time on the electro underground scene to the dizzy heights of pop stardom. While I really enjoyed my interviews with the band's backing singers, the lovely, down to earth Yorkshire lasses Joanne Caterall and Susan Sulley, I've always been fascinated by the group's lead singer, Phil Oakey, who's remained 'under the radar' for decades now.

Nobody really knows anything about him, do they? He appears on the odd music documentary. But he's managed, somehow, to stay out of the headlines completely. He's managed to keep his private life, well, totally private.

I would love to have interviewed Phil, who has one of the best voices in pop for me. But maybe his anonymity makes him even more interesting.

Clive James, the broadcaster, writer, and raconteur wasn't a bad substitute, with his quiet charisma and natural charm. Another brush with brilliance for little old me. He brought his one man show to The Lowry.

Other interviews I sadly missed was a chat with the brilliant comedian Rich Hall, a stand up famed for his gruff and deadpan delivery. My brother Jon never let me forget the time he, my dad and I went to see him at The Lowry. Hall was signing copies of his latest book in the theatre foyer, and I just froze. I couldn't bring myself to go and meet my favourite stand up. Maybe I was scared of saying something stupid.

But there is *one* interview I would have killed for – even as a freelance - the former president of South Africa Nelson Mandela. He's been my hero over the decades, and it would have been a truly inspirational experience had I been given a chance to hear his story. I would never dream of trying to equate the struggles of Mandela and his people to finally achieve freedom with mine. But theirs is a struggle that provided me with a tremendous degree of inspiration over the years.

I am agnostic when it comes to religion these days, but I wonder if Christ comes to us in the form of other people in order to teach us how to be good humans. People like Nelson Mandela.

A few years ago, I can remember being on the verge of having a blazing row with a former colleague's girlfriend who grew up in South Africa.

I asked her what she thought of Mandela. "I think he's a criminal – but you'll probably disagree." I was seething. "The only criminals involved were the ones running the appalling apartheid regime."

I even sent the ANC, the political party which Mandela led, a cheque many years ago. I sent it to their London office.

While I never got chance to interview Mandela, I spent time with a man who had in 2005. Sir David Frost asked the man who became South Africa's first black President if he felt any bitterness towards his former oppressors. Mandela simply said there was no time for bitterness as there was work to be done.

Incredible.

There's also a scene in the film Invictus which tells the compelling and moving story of what happened when the 1995 rugby World Cup came to South Africa, and it begins with Mandela being released from jail.

He's duly elected President of his country and calls a meeting of his predecessor's nervous employees at the seat of government who all assume they're about to join the ranks of the unemployed because of the colour of their skin and the fact they were complicit with the former apartheid regime.

Nelson Mandela, played so memorably by Morgan Freeman, wastes no time in quashing their fears and pledges the beginning of a sustained period of reconciliation and healing for his country.

As for Frost himself, I found he lived up to his surname and found it hard to warm to him. Surname pun definitely intended. He also appeared to be very business-like and he had an air of superiority about him. It was like he was talking to me as a favour while in reality it was to promote his one man show before it came to The Lowry.

Being a journalist is a fascinating, interesting, and stimulating job and most people do have a good story to tell.

It's important to be a good listener and observer and I feel the latter quality was one my disability helped me to cultivate because there have always been experiences that are closed to me because of my condition. Do you need to be a people person? Well, up to a point you do. Far more important is an ability to get on with all different types of people, including those you might not like very much.

For instance, there was a contact of mine at one of the amateur theatre groups in Trafford who would praise me to the skies when we gave her talentless troupe coverage and gave me hell when news items she'd given us failed to get into the paper. Explanations were futile.

I often wondered if the job also presented me with an opportunity to give something back as a disabled person to others living with disabilities. For instance, I wrote several stories on children who have cerebral palsy whose parents were fighting for funding so they could have life changing surgery. I wrote a story on a Stretford girl in 2014, who had CP and whose mum and dad were striving to raise

£25,000 to fund SDR surgery in a bid to improve her walking. It felt like I was being given an opportunity to give something back and the couple's fundraising bid, helped by the efforts of the child's army of supporters, was a success.

I wrote a similar story on a lad from Old Trafford whose parents were also battling to fund SDR treatment for their son and it attracted national attention. Kate Green, the family's MP, even raised the matter in Parliament with the then Health Secretary, Jeremy Hunt. The youngster has the same condition and his parents wanted the op for the same reason.

I certainly can't forget the story about Brentwood School in Timperley which resulted in the students over 16 – the school caters for young people with a range of disabilities – having their transport to school temporarily withdrawn. Trafford Council later overturned the decision. Result!

The money required for SDR surgery and the cash needed to help the Brentwood students was a mere drop in the ocean, really, which leads me to the conclusion that in this country of ours the powers that be, have sometimes got their priorities all wrong.

If this book comes across as one long sob story, then I've failed. I've never wanted anyone to put their arm around me and say "there, there." All I've ever wanted is for someone to say, "there you go - now show us what you can do."

At All Saints I can remember a group of pupils being asked to tidy away the chairs in the social club on a Friday afternoon. They would then be given complimentary bottles of coke which they would take great delight in holding aloft to 'toast' their jealous peers as they passed the window.

While I hated this at the time, all I've ever wanted to be was a person in *that* room looking out rather than looking in. I hope that makes sense.

While the provision to help people with disabilities get jobs is as poor and patchy as it was when I left university, I feel I succeeded despite of and not because of the system. Various organisations are useful to you if you want a menial job which seems a poor reward for my academic grind.

After leaving the Messenger I wanted a complete change in direction and wanted to use my writing skills to help make a difference, however small, to the lives of other people less fortunate than me. I've always had a strong social conscience and felt it was the right time to stop trying to put the world to rights from the comfort of my settee.

I joined the Trafford Centre for Independent Living and spent two very happy years as its volunteer publicist.

While I had to curb my sense of humour to an extent, the banter in the office was great and I felt really appreciated.

Being a 'first' isn't easy and while I've always just got on with things, thanks to my steely determination and the unwavering support of my family, I have felt lonely at times. I was the first obviously disabled student on the NCTJ course and the first journalist with a disability to be employed by the Messenger.

And, while I can't prove this, I'm pretty sure I was the first pupil with a disability at Blessed Thomas Holford Secondary School.

Before leaving CIL I came up with the bright idea of interviewing people with disabilities who I thought of as positive role models – something I found was sadly lacking when I was growing up. The idea was to tell their story and hopefully inspire others living with a disability to succeed.

I put the idea to Batir, my colleague, and he agreed.

My first and only interview I did was a Q&A with Cherylee Houston, who, like me, knew how it felt to be a 'first' when the wheelchair user became the first actress with a disability to join the cast of Britain's longest running soap, Coronation Street.

Her overriding emotion as she was about to join the Corrie cast was one of excitement, she said. Being a 'first' didn't seem to bother her at all.

Cherylee, whose cv includes appearances in the medical soap Doctors and the classic cult comedy Little Britain, was about to do one of those 'in conversation' type evenings at Sale's Waterside Arts Centre.

The event had been organised by the Standard Issue podcast. Cherylee said she was excited to be asked to play Izzy and make history back in 2010 and there was no sign of nerves at all.

I came to the conclusion that I would try to be more like Cherylee in future because there are times when nerves do still get the better of me and I struggle when it comes to embracing change as a positive thing.

Working at this organisation was stimulating, challenging and fun and it was also the first time I'd worked in the charity sector since 1988. I loved it.

Then Trafford CIL lost its funding, and I was out of work yet again. Can you be made redundant from a volunteer job?

I also did voluntary work at Henshaws, the Old Trafford charity supporting people with visual impairments and 18 months at Trafford Carers Centre as a volunteer publicist. I also did a placement in Trafford Council's press office.

I emailed the newly named RADAR charity to ask if they had any records relating to the journalism bursary scheme and they said they hadn't. I wanted to see how successful it had been.

In more than two decades working as a journalist I never came across anyone who looked like me. Hopefully it wasn't one giant waste of fucking time.

One of my fears when trying to get into journalism was that I wouldn't be able to produce as much as my able-bodied colleagues. But I can remember Phil, my Editor at the time, praising me for the sheer volume of work I *was* able to get through at one of my reporter assessments.

The key to my own success has been my own steely determination – isn't there a theory that people aren't given anything they're unable to cope with?

Equally important has been the support of my parents who always had high expectations of me. There must be so many people with disabilities languishing at home who could have achieved so much more had they been given the life opportunities I have.

Hopefully there's still the argument to be made for quality over quantity in today's high-pressured workplace.

I've always taken pleasure from writing because as I've already said, it's something I can do where my disability just doesn't matter.

My pieces never had 'by Rick Bowen who has cerebral palsy' next to them. They just had the words by Rick Bowen.

These days I spend my time trying to be the next Alan Bennett. I jest of course, as there will ever only be one Alan Bennett.

Having watched literally hundreds of plays I've decided to write some myself. Apart from 'A Long Day's Journey into a Nightmare', I've also written a short piece called 'Would You Like A Boiled Sweet?' It's a 15-minute monologue in the style of Alan Bennett's 'Talking Heads' series and is about a lonely old man who befriends a boy from the wrong side of the tracks.

It's loosely inspired by a friendship I had with an elderly neighbour called Alf who sadly died when I was in my first year at university. We would spend hours together when I was a child and later as a teenager and Alf was fascinating, a walking, talking history book who could remember things from his childhood in almost forensic detail, like how he celebrated Christmas when he was a kid, from going to Midnight Mass to the mince pies his mother made.

I also continue writing a theatre review blog – 'stagestruck.info'. Who knows, maybe after spending more than 30 years reviewing other people's plays, one day, just one day, critics will come to see one of mine.

That's my dream now and as Debbie Harry from Blondie once sang, 'dreamin' is free'.

**Listed below are some of the famous names I've
been lucky enough to interview:**

Paul Heaton – musician
Brent Sadler – former ITN war correspondent
Geraldine James – actress – Back To Life
Mark Radcliffe – radio and TV presenter
Elaine Paige – singer, actor and broadcaster
Gary Waldhorn – actor – probably best known for
playing David Horton in The Vicar of Dibley
James Fleet – actor – Hugo Horton in The Vicar of
Dibley
Andy Hamilton – writer and comedian
Marti Pellow – lead singer – Wet Wet Wet
Lorna Luft – daughter of stage and screen icon Judy
Garland
Chris Difford – musician – Squeeze
Dave Hemmingway – The Beautiful South
Paul Lake – Manchester City FC
Russell Howard - comedian
Caroline Aherne – actress – Mrs Merton/The Royle
Family
John Henshaw – actor – Early Doors
Denise Welch – actress
Tim Healy – actor
Timothy West – actor

<u>Gallery</u>

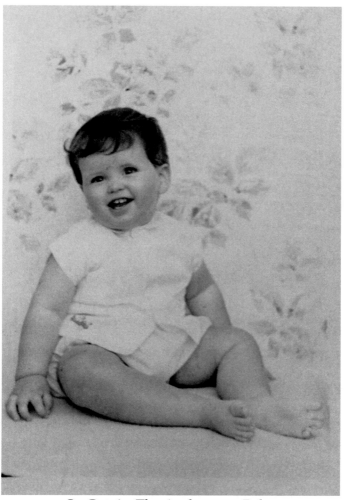

So Cute! – The Author as a Baby

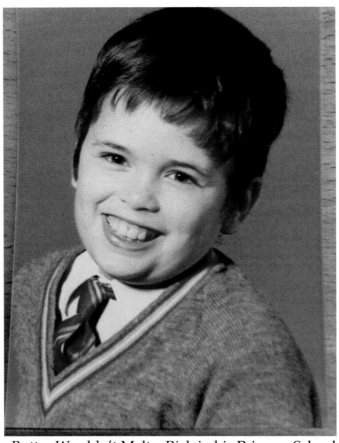

Butter Wouldn't Melt – Rick in his Primary School Uniform

Rick with Parents Margaret and Graham

Rick Having a Laugh at his University Hall of
Residence, Ranmoor House

Rick Graduates with a Degree in English Literature
from the University of Sheffield

The Best Post-Birthday Present Ever – Rick leaves home for his First Day at The Sale and Altrincham Messenger

'Come On You Blues' – Rick Pre-Match outside the
Etihad Stadium, Home of Manchester City FC

Steve Coogan
By courtesy of Baby Cow Productions

Hugh Cornwell

Midge Ure

Rosie Jones
© By kind permission of Aemen Sukkar

Sue Perkins

© Hacienda by kind permission of Ian Tilton